WOMEN AND SELF-CONFIDENCE:

How to Take Charge of Your Life

Women and Success Series:

WOMEN and SELF-CONFIDENCE:
How to Take Charge of Your Life

WOMEN AND SELF-CONFIDENCE:
How to Take Charge of Your Life

Written and Illustrated by
CAROL V. HAVEY

POSITIVE PRESS

1987

First Positive Press Printing, 1987

WOMEN and SELF-CONFIDENCE:
How to Take Charge of Your Life

Library of Congress Catalog Number 86-63909

ISBN 0-9617887-0-4

I. Title
II. Women and Success Series

Printed in the United States of America

Dedicated

. . . to all women,

. . . of all ages,

. . . everywhere.

Acknowledgments

To my husband, Bill, and to my sons, Mark, Chris, Dan, John and Kevin, my thanks for their support and encouragement.

To my daughters, Julie and Mary, both athletes and career women, and to my mother, Marynance Reedy who is a well-spring of common sense and positive attitude, thank you for being my role models and inspiration.

Most especially I thank my sister, Ann Canaday, who is not only my editor, but also my best friend.

Contents

PART IV   WORKING

PART V   GETTING IT TOGETHER

PART I
Taking Charge

1

YOU NEED TO WAKE UP

ake up to the fact that you are a terrific person with unlimited potential.

What you need is self-confidence.

How do you get it? Bit by bit. Consider the following:

It was 1972. All of my seven children were in grammar school at once. Armed with my registered nursing certificate, I applied for a part-time job in a local doctor's office. The interview at the personnel agency went splendidly, until a young assistant reached my response to "Last time employed."

"There must be some mistake; it says 1958." Upon learning that the information was correct, she gasped, wide-eyed, "You can't be serious! I can't hire you. What could you possibly do?"

Obviously, the years I had spent rearing seven children and running a household were regarded as being somewhat akin to hibernating in a cave.

It was clear to me that if she needed an explanation of the value of my work for the past 14 years, she would probably be incapable of understanding it.

Is this how society (?) viewed the time spent in performing this critical and invaluable job - as a 14 year gap in my employment record?

Disgusted, with my self-confidence at an all time low, I decided to do something about it. I re-entered college, studied on my own and acquired skills. Four years later, in 1976, I had enough confidence to start my own business.

Does that mean that taking a few classes will automatically result in self-confidence?

No, that's not what I mean, at all. Information and acquired skills are not enough. It's how you feel about yourself that makes the difference.

The transforming magic of self-confidence is inside you right now. Its discovery, release, and growth are up to you. For you who desire to increase your self-confidence, take charge of your life, and reach for your dream, this is the place to begin.

- -

Think About It

You are a unique, wonderful, valuable human being!

You have within you the seeds of greatness!

Knowing that this is true will give you the self-confidence to strive to reach your greatest potential.

You need not try to act like someone else, look like someone else, be someone else. You are YOU! You are who you want to be!

Have as your goal being the very BEST YOU you can possibly be.

Now DO Something

Take inventory of your situation, your self and your skills.

Decide what you want out of life.

Write it down.

Determine the means to get it.

Then DO something about it!

2

TAKE CHARGE OF YOUR LIFE

ake charge of your life!

Why should you? What's in it for you?

When you feel in control of your life, you are most satisfied with it.

Taking charge leads to feelings of strength and self-confidence.

Strength and self-confidence give you courage to risk new things.

Risking new things enables you to grow.

Growing empowers you to reach your greatest potential.

You can't give what you don't have.

It is only when you possess strength, self-confidence and satisfaction with your life, that you are able to give these things to others.

When you improve your own life, you become more capable of enriching the lives of those around you.

TRUST IN GOD:
BUT DON'T JUST SIT THERE,
GRAB THE OARS!

e lived in the middle of tornado
alley.

Each year it seemed the terrible storms
increased in number and ferocity. One particularly stormy spring when all our children were
very young, I was fast becoming a nervous
wreck. I found more things to worry about. Not
that worrying helped. It didn't.

I would lie awake nights, planning. What
would I do in case of fire? Hurricane? Tornado?
Air raid? How could I carry babies to safety,
and still hold toddlers' hands, so they wouldn't
run away and get lost?

Worries preyed so much on my mind that I
told my sister-in-law my concerns. She never
once implied by word or look that I was a certi-
fied nut case. She simply and solemnly promised
me that if the radio should warn of a tornado
headed in our direction, she would instantly stop

whatever she was doing to rush to help me hustle children to safety.

All it took was the knowledge that I had actively taken a positive step toward bettering my own situation. I could sleep again knowing I wasn't completely powerless.

That was the same week that I spied a cartoon drawing on a sign board in a second hand shop. It showed a scruffy character in a rowboat, and stated with large writing across the top, "Trust in God!" Below, in the waves was added, "But in the meantime, row like hell for shore!"

Things suddenly began to make sense. I had been so busy doing what I was doing, that I had overlooked the broader perspective: pray as if it's all up to God; but work as if it's all up to you.

- -

Think About It

Worry is like a rocking chair: it keeps you busy, but it doesn't get you anywhere.

While it's a good thing to have a positive attitude; that, in itself, is not enough. You've got to DO something yourself to make things better than they are!

4

TAKING CONTROL:
IF I CAN DO IT, ANYONE CAN

ragon Lady strikes again!

I just couldn't stand it. One more day completely shot. With tears choking in my throat, I came downstairs, feeling rotten.

They were all asleep then, looking like rumpled angels. My good intentions, once again, blown to bits. How could I be so mean! My throat was chronically sore from screeching.

I would open my mouth to say something sweet; and out would come vinegar. I was exhausted by the time they were ready for bed; but no sooner had everyone quieted down for the night, than I began to think about my day.

It was almost Christmas. Julie, the oldest, was eight. Mark, Chris, and Dan were seven, five and three. John and Mary, the twins, were a year and a half; and Kevin was four months old.

I felt like the meanest mother in the world. Each morning I'd get up with good intentions. I'd say to myself, "Today we'll bake cookies. I'll teach them a song or a prayer. We'll decorate for Christmas."

Then the nonsense would start. The milk hit the floor. Someone fell down the stairs. Somebody's coat was ripped. All the mittens were wet. The boots were gone . . . again. The cream of wheat boiled over on the stove. The knee patches had worn through on at least three more pairs of corduroys.

"Somebody get the door, please. Answer the phone. Catch the baby. Mop up the milk. Turn off the stove!"

I could juggle all that. What I could not take was the teasing, the needling. Only having one sister myself, I definitely was not used to living with a bunch of small boys, who delighted in whooping, pummelling each other and teasing one another mercilessly.

At my wits end, I asked our dinner guest one evening, young Father Dowling, "When do boys outgrow razzing each other?" Our new assistant pastor had several brothers; so I figured he would be an authority. My hopes were squashed, however, when he declared, "Never!" Grinning, he added, "When we all get together, we still drive my mother crazy!"

I was willing to try anything. I decided that whenever there was a fight, or serious misdemeanor, we would stop, say a prayer together, ask forgiveness and promise not to do it again. After three days, I gave it up. We had lost a whole weekend; not a lick of work got done and all we did was pray!

So I tried another tack. One day after two hours of intermittent asking, telling and coaxing our three year old to get dressed, I had had it. When he stood in the middle of the room, opened his mouth and just screamed; I thought, "Phooey with psychology!" I took a deep breath, bent over, and screamed in his ear . . . just as loud and as long as I could!

"There," I thought, "how do you like it?" His eyes popped with astonishment! And in spite of my incredibly sore throat, I was mildly pleased with his reaction.

I was desperate!

My husband, Bill, earned a living for all of us. He worked in an accounting office during the day, attended college in the evening, helped me at home, and studied when he could.

I told him I was going crazy. He said, "I know. I get frustrated, too." Not much help.

I told my mother. She said, "Dear, I think you are wonderful, just doing as well as you do."

I talked to Bill's mother. She couldn't help; but she didn't criticize me, either.

I told my friends. We laughed with each other because we were all going crazy at the same time, just in different ways.

I told my doctor. He gave me enough tranquilizers to put me in a coma, had I taken them all as prescribed. I took only a fraction, never even finishing the first prescription.

Then, on the chance that it might help, I talked to Father Dowling again. He told me something impromptu; probably never dreaming that what he said changed my whole way of looking at things. He simply said, "Don't be so hard on yourself. God is more forgiving than we are. Who knows? Given the aggravation, keeping your temper as long as you have, maybe you're a saint."

I was shocked, speechless. Whereas I expected him to chew me out for acting so mean, screaming at my children; he actually offered, "Look here, maybe you're not doing so badly, after all."

How I needed that!

Here I was, knocking myself out, trying to handle a big job, feeling "The hurrier I go, the behinder I get." I had long since given up striving for perfection. Yet tranquilizing or scolding myself did not really remedy my feeling bad, either.

After I thought about those words, I slowly began to rearrange my values. Little by little, I decided to step back, take that broader perspective, and put an end to "the tail wagging the dog".

In short, if I could not control the actions of everything and everyone around me; I could at least control my reaction to them.

It was not easy: actually taking charge of my own actions rather than merely responding to other people's needs. To take charge of my own life required that I know myself as a person, acknowledge my own needs and limitations, and give my own feelings the same respect that I accord those of other people.

Putting these ideas into practice made the difference between feeling frustrated and exasperated all the time (the tail wagging the dog) and the rich satisfying feeling of having control over my own life.

I do not mean one has to live alone to be in control of one's life. (I am still married; and five of our children still live at home.)

Feeling in charge of one's life is largely a matter of attitude. It involves self-discovery, self-esteem and self-respect. These are the first steps one must take, on the road to self-improvement and self-confidence.

- -

Think About It

Don't be so hard on yourself; you may be doing better than you think you are.

Take time out to look at your situation objectively.

Realize that you can only have control over yourself, not other people, not the whole world.

Get to know yourself, your feelings, your needs, your wants, and your limitations.

Respect yourself, your feelings, your needs, your wants, and your limitations.

5

SELF-CONFIDENCE:
YOU DESERVE IT

ouldn't it be great if all of our plans
worked successfully every time?

Nice dream, but hardly likely.

As it is, when our best laid plans get fouled
up along the way, we are forced to improve upon
the original design. Working for improvement is
the only way by which we can grow.

Of course, each person has her own view of
a situation. Take the difference between Henny
Penny and Pollyanna. Henny Penny was not only
an alarmist; she was paranoid. She ran around,
screaming about imminent disaster that was all in
her own mind.

Pollyanna, on the other hand, looked at
things optimistically. Although her friends'
attention dwelt mainly on the negative aspects of
any situation, Pollyanna concentrated only on
positive possibilities. If there were rain instead
of sunshine, she might likely say, "Aren't we
lucky to have an umbrella?"

Now, there are those who would call Pollyanna a silly little twit who couldn't recognize an obstacle if she fell over it. Not so. She recognized obstacles, all right. She just refused to be stopped by them; she was determined to turn negatives into positives.

We have a choice. We can look at the world around us, and shake our heads in despair, moaning, "Doom and gloom. Gloom and doom!" and feel powerless to act effectively. Or we can look at the same world events, and concentrate on one small area over which we can exert some measure of control.

Then, if we choose to do so, we can work toward improving the situation. By doing this, we establish confidence in our own efforts. At the same time, we set up a pattern by which we actively work to take charge of our own lives.

Instead of feeling overwhelmed by frustration and despair, we can achieve control of our circumstances if we make a conscious effort to do so.

Self-determination and self-confidence are not free, nor do they develop automatically. Like all worthwhile goals, we have to work at them.

- -

Remember

The world is not perfect. Even our best plans sometimes run amuck.

When that happens, you can either give up or go on. The choice is up to you.

If you choose to go forward, two good results are possible:

- You may find a solution to your problem.
- More importantly, you set up the personal behavior pattern of perseverance!

While solving the immediate problem is your initial concern, the real value lies in **establishing the habit of perseverance**.

6

YOU'VE COME A LONG WAY . . .

n 1960, Dr. Tom A. Dooley's primitive medical services in Laos were being criticized.

"My God, man," commented his dismayed visitor, "you're practicing 19th century medicine!" Whereupon Dooley, internationally famous American humanitarian, grinned and replied, "Well then, we've come a long way. For a 13th century country, that's not bad."

So I couldn't help but think of Tom Dooley when my husband read the first half of this book, and was visibly puzzled. "Why do you want to write a book? You have your own business; you are a professional artist and craftsperson; you write and you lecture. So do a lot of other people, but they haven't written a book about it. What is your purpose?"

"I have grown a lot, in the past fifteen years, in many ways," I answered. "I would like to share that experience in personal growth with other women. It was hard for me. I think I can make it easier for them."

"What do you mean . . . grown?" he asked. "You look the same to me."

"We can't all receive the Most Valuable Player award," I thought impatiently. Sometimes, more important is the award for Most Improved Player. I tried to explain that it was not the magnitude of my achievements that was so remarkable, but the distance that I have come since beginning.

I reminded him that only a short 15 years ago, I not only did not have any answers about surviving in the world outside my home, I did not even know the questions. Talk about a sheltered life: four years living in the nurses' residence with the Daughters of Charity of St. Vincent De Paul right after public high school, followed by marriage, and seven children in eight and a half years. Rip Van Winkle was well informed compared to me. I did not even have time to read a newspaper until Kevin (the youngest) entered school. It was only then that my head rose above babies far enough to look around and get a glimmer of how deplorably uninformed I was about financial survival and other things in the outside world.

While I was totally occupied with home and children, Bill had continued to grow and earn his way in his profession.

One becomes accustomed to life as it is. Bill has forgotten (if he ever noticed) how much my attitude and outlook have changed in the last fifteen years. I tried to explain, "When a woman feels little or no control over her life, she feels disenfranchised, powerless and helpless. Also, in a society where money is the 'bottom line', the lack of ability or opportunity to earn it on one's own leads to a devastating loss of self-esteem."

"That is silly", he scoffed. "Nobody feels like that." After a pause, "At least, no man does."

Slowly it dawned on me, "If you have never been there, how could you be expected to know?"

"Well, anyway," he continued, more mystified than ever, "why would your background and experience be valuable to other women?"

"Because I am a business professional and lecturer NOW, yet STILL AM a wife and mother with five children still at home. Mine is a unique and valuable vantage point. Not only that, I am still growing!"

- -

Keep In Mind

If you lack the ability or opportunity to earn money in a money-oriented society, you can feel helpless, powerless and frustrated.

It is a long way from this attitude to one of courage, strength and self-confidence.

You don't have to win an Olympic gold medal or an Academy Award to be a winner. Look only at your Personal Record. Anything you do to make your self and your life better than it was yesterday is an achievement you can be proud of!

Keep growing!

7

YOU CAN MAKE IT HAPPEN

t is within your power to make your life better.

If you wish this to be so, it is only YOU that can make it happen. You cannot wait for someone or something else to come along and make you more successful, richer, happier, more content, more loving, more intelligent, more beautiful than you already are. Face it. This is something YOU have to do yourself.

"Oh, sure," you say, "some people are born knowing how to succeed at everything they do." Wrong. It just seems that way because you only see their efforts that worked out well. You weren't witness to all the times they botched the job and to the experiments that didn't pan out.

While some people have more to work with than others, the fact is that we can all learn to make the most of what we have. Who do you think has a better chance for success? The person who wastes her many God given talents/advantages, or the average person who perseveres . . . who is determined to do her best and achieve her goals?

Do you sometimes feel that you have nothing to say about your life? That other people and circumstances seem to make all your decisions for you? You feel squeezed into a box and can't get out. Adrift, without direction or control, you say, "What can I do?"

What you can do is take hold of the oars, yourself! Grab them, if necessary! Take charge of your life! Start making your own decisions. Learn to take risks. Not every idea is going to work out the first time. But you can't let that stop you.

It's comfortable, in a dull sort of way, just to roll along doing what you've always done. Easier on the brain, too, and no big decisions to make. It's also a way to stagnate, to be in a rut, and to go nowhere.

What about all those dreams that you never had the opportunity to try out? It's never too late to try. It's never too late to learn. As long as you're breathing, it's never too late to grow, to develop, to improve, and to create new joy. It's never too late to begin.

It boils down to this. Look at yourself, inside and out. Are you absolutely, perfectly content with everything? Or do you want more? How do you feel? What do you want? Do you want it strongly enough to do something about it?

It is exciting and wonderful when you feel that you are going in the direction that you want to go. But you are the one who must be the doer, the pursuer. You are the only one who can, and should, control your direction. After all, it is your life. Don't be afraid to take charge of it.

Fifteen years ago I was in turmoil. I had terminal cabin fever and a vocabulary stunted by years of close association with little children. I felt hassled and worried, scared and confused. With seven children born in less than nine years, I had precious little time to socialize with adults. A parent-teacher conference was my night out.

I felt harried, as if I were being pulled in all directions at once. Furthermore, I started worrying, "What if one of us died? What if I had to take care of our children all by myself? God, what a scary thought! What ever would I do?"

I had been out of the paid work force so long, I had absolutely no confidence in myself to compete out in the big world. Then a series of events took place that frightened me into taking action. I began a determined course of self-development.

It has taken me the last fifteen years to become a professional in a field that I love, while simultaneously mothering a large family. I feel less worried about the future, because instead of merely stewing about it, I am doing something on my own to give it direction. Little by little, I have taken positive action to better my outlook, my skills, and my position.

Initiating action myself has given me a feeling of control over my own destiny. This has replaced that terrible feeling of being controlled by others and by circumstance.

For many years I did not know what it was that I sought. I only knew that I was desperately impatient to find it. It would have been easier to map my route if I had had a guide. Hindsight is always much clearer than our vision as we muddle through life. It has become clear to me only recently what it was that I was looking for: self-confidence and a feeling of control over my life.

I share with you, now, my own journey in personal growth.

- -

Take Action

YOU are the only person who can make your life better than it is.

Look at yourself with honesty:
- Are you perfectly content?
- Do you want more?
- Do you want it enough to do something about it?

Prepare yourself to:
- Learn to take risks!
- Make your own decisions!
- Take charge of your life!

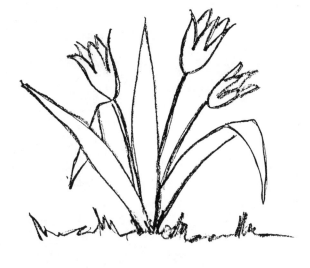

PART II
My Rainbow Journey

8

TURNING POINT:
IF I DIE, MY WORRIES ARE OVER

t all started when I brought home
Sylvia Porter's book, <u>Teach Your Wife To Be a
Widow</u>.

That got Bill's attention immediately.

That was an eventful summer. We moved
from Chicago's south side to a larger house in the
old western suburb of LaGrange, Illinois. All
seven of our children were in the same grammar
school at the same time and I was in the throes of
what seemed to be terminal cabin fever. Within
the past twelve months, the husbands of five of
my best friends had either died or left.

All of which got me to thinking, "All these
people are dying. What if I die? . . . My
worries would be over: we all have to go some-
time; I've done my best."

Then the real horror occurred to me: "What
if Bill weren't here? My God! What would I do?
How would I earn a living? How could I take
care of the family?" I did not even pay the bills,

or know what insurance we had. I was house bound to the point where going to church was a holiday.

Just about that same time, my mother decided that she might not live forever, so she divided a portion of her carefully budgeted savings between my sister and me.

Several thousand dollars were more than Bill and I had ever been able to save. Overwhelmed, I asked, "What do you want us to do with it?"

Mom replied, "That is your concern now; not mine. Make it grow."

So, of course, I asked Bill, "What shall we do with it?"

He said, "It's your money, not mine. You figure it out."

Up until then, if I wanted to purchase an item priced over $30, I would consult Bill first. (He accorded me the same courtesy, by the way.)

Also, I had always ignored both the sports and business sections of the newspaper as being completely uninteresting.

Then I discovered Sylvia Porter and Martha Patton. They each wrote regular newspaper columns on Family Finance. I looked at the photos which headed their columns and thought, "Nice, normal looking women, not too scary. I'll read their advice."

In the meantime, several of my best friends were learning about finance the hard way. With the sudden loss of their husbands, they were left with no income, with debts, small children, no work history to speak of, and no credit. One friend had a misunderstanding about insurance she thought she had (and her husband was an insurance agent). All their assets, including the house and car, were in his name. She was totally ignorant of bills, contracts and legal rights. This was all in addition to loss, killing grief, pain, total shock, and (in her case) a total loss of self-esteem.

After reading Sylvia Porter's book, I realized that, statistically, chances are pretty good that most wives are going to become widows. Like it or not, there it is.

The loss of a spouse is usually accompanied by two kinds of shocking stress: emotional and nitty-gritty everyday survival.

What to do? Appreciate the present; each precious day.

Also, equip yourself to survive, if it comes to that.

In other words, "Hope for the best, but prepare for the worst."

One of Sylvia's first recommendations was for sufficient life insurance. Martha Patton feels that "sufficient" life insurance is the amount necessary to tide the family over until the surviving spouse is capable of taking over the job of provider, whether that includes completing college, or whatever.

I figured if worst came to worst, and something were to happen to Bill (God forbid), I would be in dire straits just handling my emotions and caring for the children. It would be a heck of a time to embark upon school re-entry and career building, starting at rock bottom. However, if I could begin learning survival skills now, it would relieve some of the pressure later on. (Besides, if nothing happened to Bill, I would still have all those fine skills to enjoy for our mutual benefit.)

51

Think About It

If your husband is the sole breadwinner and tragedy should strike (God forbid):
- Are you employable?
- Could you make a living?
- Are you capable of supporting your family?
- Are you thoroughly familiar with all your insurance policies, bills, mortgage?
- Do you save money regularly?
- Do you know how to invest your money wisely?

If the answer is "no" to several of these questions, you may be living dangerously.

9

A PLAN:
ACQUIRE SURVIVAL SKILLS

ow that I had goals (to acquire survival skills), I listed steps by which I might attain them.

1. Resume education to improve job skills.
2. Acquire credit in my own name; and as much as possible.
3. Arrange to have family assets in each of our names in equal amounts. (In many instances, joint ownership is legally considered HIS ownership, since HE earned the money to buy it.)
4. Acquaint myself personally with banker, insurance agent, stock broker, auto mechanic, and real estate broker, etc.

It soon became apparent that these valuable and worth-while goals were going to require other things: my time, my energy, and my family's understanding and support.

Since there were still only 24 hours in a day, I decided that, in order to have time to embark upon this new self-improvement plan, I would have to eliminate some of my other activities. It boiled down to one initial factor: if a task was urgent and necessary for family well-being, it got done . . . otherwise, it didn't.

Second decision: whose job was it to perform these tasks "urgent and necessary for family well-being?" Everyone's and anyone's, depending on who was capable and who was available.

Everyone was going to have to share the responsibility as equally as possible. This usually meant that if I was the only one who could possibly accomplish a job, I did it. Otherwise, the job got delegated. Since there was always a full day's worth of jobs which only I could perform, the children had plenty of chores.

Another very real problem was energy. I had very little. Flat feet, a naturally low energy level and a body in need of repair left me easily exhausted. (I had had seven children, including emergency Caesarean twins, and a ruptured ectopic pregnancy in eight and one half years.)

How is a person going to be enthusiastic about adding new ventures to an already full schedule, when she feels "done in" by noon? Again, I learned from my children who are track and long distance runners. They not only do well in studies (so did I), but they all strive to stay fit.

"Sorry, Mom, can't scrub the kitchen now; I'm due at cross-country practice. Gotta stay in shape, you know. Can't grocery shop now, Mom; gotta finish lifting weights." They showed good sense. A sound mind and a healthy body are worth working for. "And look at me," I thought. "I'm in worse shape than anybody.

This is one job I cannot delegate. I'll have to do it myself."

First of all, I elected to have the repair surgery that I had been putting off for years. What a change. By the end of that year, I could actually walk a block without fearing that I would come apart at the seams. I even got brave enough to learn how to ride a two-wheeler (with a runner ahead of me, shouting, "Run for your lives! She can't steer!").

Having accomplished this great feat, I was encouraged to jog to the end of the block. Thought I would die! But I didn't. So the next day, I jogged all around the block! The family thought I had gone crazy, but they all applauded.

Actually, I surprised myself and wondered if I could do more. Much more like the tortoise than the hare, I jogged every morning for the next two years, before going to a running sports podiatrist. I told him, whereas "my feet have always hurt up to my neck", now I could pinpoint where they hurt most. After a while he fitted me with soft orthotics (removable shoe inserts). After all these years, it not only didn't hurt to stand, I actually felt like running around!

All my life, I thought everybody's feet and legs hurt; that they were just braver than I, that I must be a panty waist. What a revelation! It was terrific. I also discovered that, "ladies'" clothing often rides up or down, binds, and otherwise inhibits full range of motion, whereas proper running attire fits comfortably, stays put, and permits ease of motion for full body activity.

Whee! Where had I been hiding? How had I missed out on all these great things? Soon my permanent footwear became a good pair of running shoes. My clothing I designed for fit, ease and comfort as well as for color and attractiveness. And the family soon got used to my morning run. "I'm off for my run now. Have the dishes done by the time I get back. Gotta stay in shape, you know."

Understanding and support are reciprocal things: you get what you give. The more I became involved with my classes, the more aware I became of my children's difficult work and fine efforts. When I started back to school, they related to my class efforts instantly. Arriving home from school, they would ask, "How is it going, Mom? Got your homework done? What's that project you're working on? How'd the test go? You want me to quiz you for it?" And when I would talk about school, they would listen.

Conversely, when one of them had three term papers and four finals all in the same week, I was aghast; and told him or her, "Now you go study. I'll bring you some hot tea and call you when supper's ready, you poor thing."

The encouragement in sports that we always gave the children, they returned to me. You don't need to come in first to be a winner. I entered three 5 Kilometer races in my life and came in last, or close to it, in all. But that is all right; I finished! And lived to tell the tale! My whole family was there to cheer me on and celebrate the victory of participating. Any time any of us better a personal record (P.R.), we all frankly share and applaud the effort and the victory as "a job well done".

Bill's understanding and support was essential in all this, too. Looking back, I think, at first, he did not pay much attention to my concern about self-improvement. Perhaps, later, he tolerated my efforts or was mildly interested and amused. When he noticed my increased commitment to school, rearrangement of household chores and my new focus, I think, perhaps, he felt annoyed . . . maybe even threatened.

About then he started making noises like, "A woman's place is in the house." To which I would quietly reply, "And in the Senate."

I decided that whatever I had to do, I would do willingly and cheerfully. And if I couldn't bring myself to be willing and cheerful, I wouldn't do it. It took six years or so to progress from "Yes sir, no sir, you know best sir" to "No-o-o, please?" to " No, because . . ." to "No, thank you" to just plain "No."

I had to learn to incorporate several ideas firmly into my way of thinking:

1. Everybody has feelings; you do not have to apologize for feelings.
2. Nobody is a mind reader.
3. If you really want something:
   a. You must <u>decide</u> **exactly** what it is.
   b. You must <u>plan</u> how to get it.
   c. You must <u>work</u> for it.

Having established this, I figured I had better keep Bill posted. So I regularly shared my feelings, whether he was much interested or not. At first, I was not sure how to go about all this education business or where it would lead exactly; but I was sure that I had to do something.

He sometimes did not agree with my choices. But I believe I earned his respect with my effort

59

and hard work. With time, my judgment, as well as my skills, improved. The more I learn of business, the more I admire and appreciate Bill's high level of skill and the magnificent job he has done, and is doing, supporting this whole family.

His attitude toward my learning now is rather like our attitude toward the children's schooling. If you are doing it for self enrichment, fine. If it is a tool for earning, use it.

It is, more or less, a family encouragement to "Fish, or cut bait." If you want to do something, don't just sit there thinking about it - DO IT! And if it doesn't work out; well, at least you've given it your best shot. You can always try something else.

- -

Use This Book for Moral Support

Do your family and friends offer no support? No encouragement? Well, so what!

Whose life is it, anyway? You're the one who has to live it. No one else.

If being your own person is new to you, your family and friends might as well get used to it. If your decision to become an independent woman who strives for excellence comes as a shock to them, TOO BAD!

Don't let other peoples' lack of enthusiasm discourage you! This is important!

Think about it. If some people see your new involvement in striving for excellence as a personal inconvenience to them, it's not surprising that they may even be dismayed by your new enthusiasm.

If these are people you really care about, you must patiently try to show them that this is not just a whim, a passing fancy: you're serious about improving your life.

On the other hand, if the people who make discouraging noises at you are strangers or mere acquaintances, just don't give them another thought.

After all, it has been so long since some people have entertained a new idea, they wouldn't know what to do with it if they had one.

10

CONTINUING EDUCATION:
LUCILLE, COME BACK; I'M NOT FINISHED

ith the youngest child in school full time, I thought, "Now's the time to further my own education."

With a three year Registered Nursing diploma, 15 years after graduation, I would need more than a refresher course to begin nursing again. My one brief year in nursing had been spent in the clinic and Emergency Room at the hospital in which I trained, St. Joseph's in Chicago, Illinois.

St. Joseph's now has a new facility on Lake Shore Drive. Our building, at 2100 North Burling, was so old that it was condemned right after our class graduated. Built before The Great Chicago Fire of 1871, it barely escaped destruction when the inferno stopped at the end of the block.

My biggest problem (besides sore feet and legs) always seemed to be organizing my work to get everything accomplished in a HURRY! You might wonder, then, about my working in the

E.R. That fact puzzles our oldest daughter, Julie, too. She's now an R.N. in the surgical intensive care unit at Loyola Medical Center. She's very good, very organized and very FAST! My slowness drives her crazy and she knows I dislike being interrupted when I'm working. Actually, at that time, St. Joseph's didn't have too many emergencies. I remember being on call one night, and hearing the switchboard operator on the public address system paging every intern and resident in the whole place. I thought, panic stricken, "It must be a fire! Maybe a train wreck!" Racing to the E.R. and finding no one, I called the main desk. The pizza had arrived!

In any case, I decided that if my legs didn't like standing ten hours a day on a tile floor when I was nineteen, they'd like it even less now. However, a Bachelor of Science degree might provide me with a wider choice of jobs, perhaps something wherein I could sit down occasionally and not feel like I was racing all the time.

After spending an entire summer getting transcripts untangled, I found, to my dismay, that my three year hospital program (in which I earned just about straight A's) counted for nothing toward a degree. Because the courses were not conducted on a university campus, they were worth ZIP. Before I would be permitted to take any further classes, I would be required to pass the final exams in all my previous classes. This, of course, would mean studying each subject all over again and paying for it a second time, too. That was too much.

If I had to start from scratch, I'd be darned if I'd repeat myself. There must be other interests and talents I could discover within myself to build upon. So, I thought I'd begin by taking a class or two with our local Adult Education program. The first class I signed up for was tailoring, and the first thing I learned was that I had signed up for the wrong class. I had hoped to learn short cuts in sewing, but apparently requesting short cuts from a French tailor is like ordering a ham sandwich in a Jewish deli. It just isn't done. Furthermore, our instructor, a talented (but insecure) French woman had a pronounced accent. She had begun her sewing career at age 13 at a Parisian haute couture. Her first project at that age was a lined, wool, princess-style coat with 32 bound buttonholes!

I, on the other hand, knew very little about tailoring. Why else would I have taken the class? Being a slow worker, I needed to ask questions. We had no written instructions, of course, only her verbal ones. The problem was that when anyone asked her to repeat, she became very angry, snapping that her accent was being ridiculed. We slow students, therefore, were just plain stuck. I finished a suit jacket and camel colored wool coat, but don't know to this day if they were done according to her instructions. And I'm not about to ask, either.

I was delighted when another opportunity to learn tailoring presented itself. My neighbor's sister, Lupe, from Cuernavaca, Mexico, came to visit her. While Lupe was here, she made lovely, imitation fur coats for each of her two nieces, without a pattern. I asked her how she did it. She showed me several knotted strings. She indicated that she took measurements using these strings and cut her fabric pieces accordingly.

65

This skill blew my mind. Could she teach me how to do it? Sure. Only one small problem: communication. Guadalupe spoke only Spanish, I spoke only English, and my neighbor Maria (our interpreter) did not sew. So much for Mexican pattern drafting.

Shortly thereafter, there was a five minute sewing show on television. Lucille Rivers (not to be confused with a comedienne) was a well-known American fashion designer, and would give pattern/designing/sewing hints sandwiched between commercials every day at noon. The remaining three minutes yielded just enough information to get me into trouble, but not enough to get me out. Each day would find me frantically screaming at my T.V., "Lucille, come back! I'm not finished."

Knowing this, you can imagine how grateful I was to discover a new course beginning at our local Junior College of Du Page: Fashion Design, Pattern Drafting 101. My sanity would be saved! (If only the instructor spoke English . . . slowly.)

- -

It's Never Too Late

Even if the need is not urgent now, examine your resources. Do you already have a profession? Are your skills up to date?

Do you know what sort of work you'd like to do? Do you need more training or education for the job you want? If so, how much? How long would it take?

Is the fact that you'd be 50 years old when you finish college holding you back? What can you lose? You'll be 50, anyway - or 70 or 90!

11

RE-ENTERING COLLEGE:
JUST TAKE OFF YOUR JACKET AND HOLD STILL

riving through a mid-winter blizzard
to Glen Ellyn's College of DuPage, I headed for
my first real college class in 16 years.

I was nervous.

My Fashion Design class was to be held in
one of the original farm buildings that was on the
land when C. O. D. bought the place. Only in
existence for several years, the college simply
erected new prefabricated buildings as they were
needed.

Actually, the pattern drafting class was in
the second story loft; the first floor housed a life
drawing class. I remember my dismay when we
were told we'd have to bundle up in our coats to
traipse over to the adjacent building if we wanted
to use the washroom during our four hour class.
How primitive! And this was the 1970's. I could
be grateful, at least, that I was not the nude
model for the life drawing class downstairs. The
building had no hallway and inefficient heat (it all

went upstairs). Every time a student opened the door, the model turned blue!

I asked many questions in Fashion Design, "What design lines would you use to de-emphasize a full figure? Large hips? No waist? Short legs?" "Tsk, tsk," my fellow students would admonish me, "You musn't put yourself down like that."

This made me realize that I already knew something that they weren't yet aware of. The final garment should create an optical illusion, it should make the wearer appear taller, thinner or whatever. The drawing room is the time for truth. Perhaps their lack of perception in this area was due to their lack of need. Most of my classmates were 19, slim and pretty; they looked good in anything. I, on the other hand, had to be selective. I wanted to know, not only what design lines to establish, but also, why certain ones created a particular illusion and how I could control those illusions at will.

One of our classes held in the farmhouse was Fashion Illustration. It was such fun that I encouraged our daughter Julie (a high school junior at the time) to take it with me. At one point, our instructor, Bette Anderson, couldn't help remarking upon my attitude. She watched me drawing, chuckling and humming to myself, and said, with a giggle, "You just LOVE what you're doing, don't you?" I answered, with surprise, "Are you kidding? I haven't had this much fun in years! I can even do it at home and truly say, 'Don't bother me now, kids, I'm doing my homework!'"

Bette commented that it appeared I'd had previous drawing classes. That was true, but it was a hundred years ago, when I was in grammar school. I had won a scholarship to the School of the Art Institute of Chicago when I was ten. If the person's work merited, s/he could earn additional scholarships at S.A.I.C. or at the Academy of Fine Arts. I was fortunate enough to do just that for several years; until I stopped, merely because I tired of it. What an idiot!

Now, years had passed since I had done much drawing. It occurred to me that, in order to do good fashion illustration, one must be familiar, not only with the clothing, but also with the body beneath. Oh yes, I was acquainted with anatomy as a nurse, but only from the standpoint of what happened when things went awry beneath the skin. Therefore, it seemed like a good idea to sign up for a life drawing class to get a view of the outside of a whole healthy body, for a change. Besides, the new life drawing class met in a building which had indoor plumbing and double doors.

In life drawing class I discovered three very exciting things:

First, I always finished my assigned drawings way ahead of my fellow students. At first, this disturbed me; I thought I must have misunderstood the directions, or that my drawings were incomplete. But, no; I just had the talent for working fast. Imagine! ME! The FASTEST one in ANYTHING!

Second, during the break, the models would always ease stiff muscles by stretching and strolling around to see our drawings. Invariably, they asked permission to have one of mine. I was so pleased. But curious. I looked at the other drawings, too. Mine were as good as any, and better than most, as far as skillful rendering goes. But some of the others, interesting though they were, seemed almost cruel to me. At times the model would appear to be gaunt, haggard or out of shape. Somehow, my drawings always showed the models as they appeared to my eyes, beautiful. I achieved good likenesses (that's a skill, in itself); but beyond that, I realized that I saw something else that the others did not see. This face, this body, this person in front of me was a rare, unique, beautiful person. I still see people that way.

The third wonderful thing I discovered in this class was a camaraderie and kindness in the other students, despite our age differences. On my first day in class, I was the last one to arrive. A quick glance told me that there were no available seats by the other suburban ladies in the rear of the room. The only place left was at a table with a pale, undernourished, pigtailed, mustached 18 year old, wearing a hand-painted "Grateful Dead" black undershirt. "My gosh," I thought, "What'll we talk about for three hours? What could we possibly have in common?" Then, I thought, with a sigh, "He's probably just as thrilled to see me." So, I broke the ice and Bob and I laughed and chatted quietly all during the drawing class.

Several weeks later, in another building, I heard someone call my name. (It couldn't be me, I thought, the halls are full of hundreds of milling young students, but nobody knows me.) I turned; and saw Bob, pigtail flapping, running after me. He had seen me go by, remembered that I had been absent from class the week before, and was afraid I might not be aware that class had been cancelled for the present week. He ran a full city block, with an armload of heavy books, to catch up with me, to tell me - to save me an unnecessary trip. Who said there had to be a generation gap? Kind people are kind people.

We students were not the only learners in that class. Our instructor, John Lemmon, a handsome, bearded, young man, strolled in one day to tell us that, since the model hadn't shown up, we could take the day off. He wasn't well-acquainted with the older members of his class. We told him that we had changed appointments, hired baby sitters, and driven 30 miles just to be there. If he couldn't find a model, . . . "Just take off your jacket and hold still!" We'd use him. He ran out into the hall and hired a passing student. (We housewives are a feisty lot!)

- -

Insights

We all have something in common. Concentrate on these similarities rather than on our differences.

When you meet someone for the first time, make a conscious effort to discover something admirable about that person or perhaps something that you have in common.

By doing this, you will find yourself so interested in other people that you don't have time to think about you. You will understand people better. You'll like people more.

12

DOES YOUR HUSBAND KNOW?

"Does your husband know you're asking all these questions?"

The insurance agent eyed me suspiciously. He didn't have to say it. I know he suspected me of slipping cyanide into the "master's" soup.

Because a woman's survival depends, to a large extent, on her ability to cope financially, she can be terribly handicapped when she is thrown on her own, especially if she has had no previous experience.

What to do? Don't wait until sudden tragedy forces you into a crash course in economics. If you're not already familiar with all the aspects of your financial survival, do what you can to remedy the situation without delay.

This was Sylvia Porter's advice. It sounded good. So, I signed up for a course in Consumer Economics, which turned out to be a real eye opener.

Among other things, we were told to:

1. Find out what your financial position is

right now.

2. Set your goals for the future.
3. Decide what you'll need to do to achieve these goals.
4. Take responsibility for your own affairs:
   a. Establish credit in your own name.
   b. Read your own financial policies (insurance, mortgage, etc.) and ask questions until you understand them.
   c. Meet your professional people personally.
   d. Comparison shop for both goods and services.

Although hesitant at first, I soon warmed to the task. It's amazing how alarmed people get when a woman begins to make herself aware.

1. Find out what your financial position is right now.

   "Why this sudden interest in insurance policies, mortgage, and social security? Do you know something I don't know? Am I sick and you're not telling me? WHAT?" asked my husband, Bill.

2. Set goals for the future.

   I found out that my primary goal and my husband's were quite different. My goal was to have enough money saved to be able to pursue my many interests and be able to travel a bit. "I don't have any hobbies," Bill said. "My goal is to stay home, follow you around with a clip board all day and instruct you on how to do your housework properly."
   "Joke or no joke," I told him, "if that's what you've got in mind, keep working."

3. Decide what you'll need to achieve those

<u>goals.</u>
What with inflation and all, we both
decided that we would need as much as
we could possibly accumulate and
comfortably invest.

4. <u>Take responsibility for your own affairs.</u>

    a. Establish credit in your own name.
Would you believe a widow in our
class had kept her husband's death
a secret for 15 years? All credit
was in his name. She was terrified
that her gas, electricity, water, and
credit would be turned off if her
creditors ever learned of his death.
I went right home, applied for three
credit cards in my own name, and
got them. (I always pay the bills
before any finance charges accrue.)

    b. Read your financial policies.
Question anything which does not
appear to be clear. I discovered
that one of our insurance policies
stated something not to our benefit.
When I asked about it, I was told,
"Oh, that's just standard formality.
It really doesn't matter." Baloney!
We changed insurance companies.

    c. Meet your professional people per-
sonally.

        1.) Seeking MEDICAL personnel had
always been my responsibility.

        2.) The others, I had left to Bill,
up until then: AUTO SALES-
MEN and MECHANICS, for example. Actually, Bill was
quite grateful for my new

interest. "This is great," he said. "I don't understand much about cars, and I always feel stupid asking questions. This way, you can ask all the questions. They won't mind explaining it to you because they won't expect you to know anything. Then you can explain it to me." He was quite right. They didn't expect me to know anything. They did explain. And I, in turn, explained it to Bill. It worked out fine.

3.) One's ACCOUNTANT, of course, is of vital importance to one's financial well-being. Now here I am in luck, as Bill is a C.P.A. Very handy when I want to meet with my accountant personally.

4.) As his own work requires long hours, Bill has little time to do REPAIR WORK on our nearly-a-century-old Victorian home. As a result, I am the one who solicits bids for repairs . . . an instructive, useful experience. I watch, ask questions, keep records, and learn for the next time. I also note the name of the particular repair man, and exactly what he repaired, for future reference.

5.) From BANKERS I received the

most wistful response. "I wish **my** wife would take an interest in **our** financial affairs," said one. "I'm not getting any younger," said another, "but she just doesn't want to hear about it."

6.) INSURANCE AGENTS were, by far, the most infuriating. In order to comparison shop for insurance and obtain the most efficient kind, I had to know exactly what their policies offered. But as soon as I began my inquiries, I received suspicious looks and blatant demands, "Does your husband know you're asking all these questions?" As if I were sneaking around behind his back! Planning to do away with him!
Really now. And this was in 1975.

- -

It's Never Too Early

Don't wait until the monsoon strikes before fixing the hole in the roof. Likewise, don't wait until you're thrown on your own to make yourself capable of standing on your own two feet.

You can't count on someone else always being there to hold your hand. There will come a time when you have ONLY YOU. So prepare yourself now! Don't delay!

Learn to stand up for yourself. And if the world isn't ready for that, that's just tough. Say to yourself, "World, look out! I'm coming through!"

13

SAVE ONE, SCRAP THE OTHER

In addition to the required courses for a degree, I elected to take a variety of studio art classes.

In Ceramics I, I was shown how to knead clay and push it into serviceable, beautiful shapes, how to fire it, and how to glaze it. Having completed these tasks sufficiently, I was told that I was ready for the big time, Ceramics II, throwing clay on the wheel.

Never have I worked so long and so hard, and accomplished so little!

I was later told that it sometimes takes as long as two years to master working on a potter's wheel. I wonder if that estimate was considerably stretched to make me feel better about my bungling attempts to succeed at this most difficult task.

Ceramics I and II were electives in the wide array of studio art courses. Even though I had never tried it, I thought blithely, "Everyone takes ceramics. How hard could it be?" We even had electric wheels, rather than those run merely by a foot pedal. This was going to be fun.

The idea was to slam the clay down hard onto the center of the flat, spinning surface. Then with the fingers, palms and heels of the hands, gently press and mold the slowly spinning wet clay into the desired shape.

I watched the other students work: smooth thin bowls, graceful containers and delicate jars magically formed under their hands. I could hardly wait to begin.

On the second day, having kneaded the air bubbles out of my clay sufficiently, I found my assigned wheel, and prepared to work my own magic.

Toward the end of the four hour class, my off-centered clay flew from the spinning wheel and landed with a sodden thwack against the hot radiator over by the wall . . . again.

This time the instructor couldn't ignore it. He came over, peered at me and patted me gently on the shoulder. I looked up, startled to see him there. I had been concentrating so on the clay, that I had become oblivious to all else.

I remembered my father telling me never to try to make a living playing poker as my emotions were always too plain to see. From the look on the instructor's face, I believe he must have thought I was about to cry.

"Oh well," I thought, "just wait until next week. I'll get the hang of it then."

Next week arrived. The first assignment was to make a plate. I did. Happily, I scratched my name in straight lines on the under-surface. The plate cracked in two.

When shaping the clay, you press it into the desired form while scraping off the excess, or that part which is not symmetrical.

The second assignment was a bowl. I thought that a huge bowl, large enough in which to serve spaghetti to the whole family, would be fine. When I scraped off the pieces that were not symmetrical, all I had left was a small saucer.

The instructor showed us various ways to make lids for our containers. Taking advantage of the opportunity to offer me a word of encouragement, he smiled, "These are nice little lids. Where are your containers?"

Crestfallen, I replied, "Those ARE my containers."

He then demonstrated several ways to make handles, a requirement for passing the class. At the end of the quarter, he reviewed my work: a small row of pitiful, lumpy, little bowls. Groping for some constructive criticism, he said, "These are nice cups. But where are their handles?"

"They are oriental tea bowls?" I shrugged helplessly.

He gave me a passing grade. I think he did not want me to repeat the class. I took the hint. I did not sign up for Ceramics III.

My sister, Ann, who loves me dearly, later looked at my frumpy bowl collection. I hid a smile, imagining her mind racing, desperately trying to think of a comment that would be positive, but sincere.

Then turning one particularly ugly bowl upside down, she grinned delightedly, "I just love the way you signed your name!"

I scrapped the bowls, and saved the logo.

- -

Make a Decision

If something interests you, try it.

Give it your best shot with enthusiasm.

If it doesn't work out well at first, and if you are still highly motivated to succeed at the particular task, persevere wholeheartedly.

Evaluate your situation. Then continue to reevaluate it regularly.

Periodically, look over your involvement in any given project with the object in mind of making a decision.

This is important. Mental hospitals are filled with people who have become incapable of making decisions.

How do you come to a decision? You determine the possible cost and the probable gains. Then ask yourself, "How much do I want this thing? Can I afford it? Am I willing to pay the price in terms of time, energy, money, etc?" Each of these is a valuable commodity!

If, at some point, the gain is no longer worth the cost to you, cut your losses, salvage what you can and get out!

You always have three possible choices: to continue, to become even more involved, or to stop.

Some people mistakenly think that they can get away without ever making decisions. Not true. If a person is already involved with something, and does nothing to change the situation, the very fact that she continues to be involved is, in itself, a decision.

The old adage which admonishes us to finish what we start is not always good advice. If you decide the goal is no longer worth your continued effort, leave it.

Count the time spent as a valuable learning experience; then move on to bigger and better things!

14

UNACCUSTOMED AS I AM . . .

nce I got used to the idea of attending college, I decided I may as well earn credit for it, too.

At the rate of only one or two classes at a time, even a two year degree looked eons away. So, I sought ways to garner the greatest amount of credits in the least amount of time.

This led to my discovery and use of C.L.E.P. (College Level Examination Program) exams and the method of earning college credits by proving proficiency to the class instructor. This second way usually meant successfully taking the final exam without benefit of having attended the classes . . . all done with special permission of the instructor, of course.

One of the classes I desired to handle in this manner was Speech Communications, worth five quarter credit hours. The final assignment was a ten minute speech, to be given while standing in front of the classroom. The day for my speech was set for the following Monday; and I confidently set about writing my notes.

Two friends agreed to hear me give it a practice shot the Friday before. As a result, to make a sad story short, they suggested that I take the class.

Embarrassed and appalled at my own ineptitude, I rewrote, polished and practiced that speech for 48 hours until blast-off time Monday morning.

Though I would not have wanted to know my blood pressure reading at the time, I did give the speech, lived to tell the tale and even passed the class. Much to my great relief and surprise, except for the professor (who was blind) and me, the classroom was empty!

In any event, this had been my sterling public speaking record when I was approached by the president of the Hinsdale Embroiderers' Guild, which I had joined the year before. "Our program speaker can't come next week so we are having our own members fill in," she said. "You can talk about fashion design and embroidered clothing for a few minutes, can't you? It's very informal. Everybody's participating. There will be four 15-minute speakers."

Trembling, and with much misgiving, I answered, "Well, sure, if you think I can."

"Oh, you'll do just fine," she responded breezily.

She called me again late Sunday night. This time she said, "One of the other speakers can't make it . . . awfully sick. You can stretch out your talk to half an hour, can't you? I know you'll be just wonderful."

"No problem," I mumbled, thinking misera-
bly, I can't back out now. They are already
going to kill me for being such a bumbling speaker for 15 minutes. What's another 15?

What to do? I called for advice from a
speaker used to handling the most difficult audience in the world. I called my friend, Diana, a
sixth grade teacher. Her advice: "Keep moving,
and give them plenty of colorful things to look
at."

That night, my husband and I both worked
long hours at our nine-foot kitchen table: he,
with our income taxes, and I, with design notes.

On Monday morning, I set off for guild with
my folder full of notes, three aspirin, and two
suitcases of embroidered clothing which I had designed.

The business portion of the meeting was over
and I had finished serving the cookies, as I was
social chairman that year. (Social chairman means
kitchen duty.) This was it. My turn next!

I must describe my audience. Never have I
met a more talented, skillful, knowledgeable,
dignified, gracious, friendly group of stitchers in
my life. There will never be a speaker who
doesn't have at least several people in this audience more experienced in any subject than she is
herself. They are, in two words, very good.

As you can see, I was, and still am, in awe
of this talented group of women. Therefore, you
can understand my dismay when I pulled out my
notes only to discover that, instead of fashion
designs, all I had was our income tax records.
(Goodness knows what my C.P.A. husband had in
HIS briefcase.)

With my bravest smile, I explained that I was reminded of the time I spoke in front of my high school English class when I had used washable ink for my notes. My hands perspired so much that all I had left when I got up to speak were midnight-blue dribbles on my index cards. I then confessed the mix-up of my notes, explaining that I would be speaking extemporaneously.

When discussing fashion, one strives at all times to use tactful words and phrases designed to conjure visions of beauty. So, it is not surprising that at one point in my talk, I became a bit tense.

I was explaining the advantage of certain types of bodice darts. Certain designs would be complimentary to one kind of figure, whereas a person with an entirely different build would be more flattered by another design.

I first described the slim and willowy Audrey Hepburn's attractive wardrobe from the famous film "Sabrina". Then, using the opposite body type for my example, I tried to think of the tactful words Jane Russell used in her Playtex brassiere commercials. Desperately replaying the television advertisement in my mind, I could envision Jane, holding forth her shapely bra, crooning, "Now, as we (full-figured) girls would say, . . ."

Just then, seeing me redden and grope for words, a helpful voice from one of the most reserved, dignified, majestic-figured members piped up from the back row, "You mean when you've got big boobs!"

Well that was it. The tension broke. Everyone howled and gone was my need to strive for extreme dignity.

After I finished, I was astonished to receive all sorts of compliments from my fellow members. "Why, I didn't know you knew all that, I learned a lot." "That was one of the liveliest programs we've had all year."

All in all, I learned how to organize a speech. More importantly, I learned that keeping your audience's attention and being entertaining can be as important as being informative.

- -

Be Ready for Opportunity . . . Then Take It

Bravely go after what you want.

Prepare thoroughly for any big job. There is no substitute for preparation.

Once you are prepared, reach out and seize opportunity when it comes near.

Assured that you are thoroughly familiar with your material, assume that your audience likes you.

On that assumption, whether speaking to a group or to prospective employers, greet them with a smile, as you would friends.

Be enthusiastic.

Take your subject seriously, but not yourself. If you make an error, have the grace, the confidence and the good humor to laugh at yourself. This puts others at ease.

When someone compliments you on a job well done, smile and have the courtesy to merely say, "Why, thank you."

15

PAID IN FULL

In grammar school I used to draw my classmates' portraits on notebook paper.

I loved the life drawing classes at the School of the Art Institute in downtown Chicago and at the Academy of Fine Art, where I had earned scholarships year after year. Of course, that was a hundred years ago, when I was ten to fourteen years old.

So, I was really surprised when I began college drawing classes in my late thirties and found that I not only hadn't lost my skill, but had become, in fact, better.

Therefore, when the women's club in my parish announced their upcoming biennial bazaar and called for volunteers, I answered without giving myself time to be properly scared. "Why certainly," I piped, "I can draw on-the-spot portraits."

"Wonderful!" the chairman said, delighted at the prospect of something a little out of the ordinary. "It's definite, then. We'll be counting on you."

What had I done? Now I was committed. Practice. Practice, that's the thing. I practiced drawing people's portraits until my face seemed permanently black with smeared charcoal. My family posed for me. My neighbors, with whom I played bridge, posed for me. The seventh graders who used the school library on Wednesday afternoon (the time that I volunteered) posed for me.

Finally, my drawings became pretty fair. Then on the first weekend of November, the big day arrived.

What if I sat there all day, and nobody wanted my services? I'd die of embarrassment. Absolutely die!

So I set up a display board with all the family portraits, put up a price sign of $1.00, and set out an appointment sheet, leaving a name space for every 15 minute interval from 9:00 a.m. through 2:45 p.m. That way, I reasoned, I could manage to look busy.

By 9:05 a.m., the appointment list was full! In the next six hours, I drew 24 charcoal portraits (my best work to date, thank God). The chairman was pleased. An unanticipated after effect, however, was that it took two glasses of wine and three hours for my hands to stop shaking. I was really dumb to put myself under the gun of a time limit like that, but how was I to know that that many people would want my drawings?

For the next bazaar, I volunteered to draw portraits again. This time I tripled my prices and omitted the appointment sheet. Success!

After that, I got brave enough to enter the LaGrange Craft Fair which takes place annually on the main street of our village. My prices went up to $7.50 and people still bought my work.

I remember a conversation with Bill, wherein I told him that going to school was very important to me because it was building my self-confidence, of which I had none.

"You have no self-confidence, huh?" he said seriously. "If I make a mistake, I do it in the privacy of my office. And in the privacy of my office, I can correct that mistake. On the other hand, you perform your skill out on LaGrange Road. If you make a mistake, you do it in front of God and everybody . . . THAT takes guts!"

No payment for drawing portraits could ever be worth more to me than that tribute.

- -

Be Realistic

Be as realistic as possible, not only in setting your goals, but also in establishing their time frame. You want success, not frustration.

16

DRAWING CAN BE HAZARDOUS
TO ONE'S HEALTH

ortraits of houses are a lot like portraits of people: they are all special and all
unique.

I learned, however, that drawing portraits
of homes and village scenes can be hazardous to
one's health and well-being.

I started out drawing pictures of homes on
site. The weather was pleasant, the streets
fairly empty. But as the seasons changed, I
realized that a body could get frostbitten or run
over doing that.

Plan B called for the use of an instant print
camera, enabling me to draw from a photograph
instead. One request led to another and I soon
had quite a few jobs.

The camera work, itself, was not difficult;
however, I learned that each occupation has its
hazards. Taking an interesting perspective shot
of train tracks disappearing in the distance, I got
hit on the head by a crossing gate. While

photographing a widow's home, preparatory to creating a surprise gift, I was reported to the local police. Her watchful neighbor, a police lieutenant's wife, noticed a "suspicious character" (me) lurking about.

The last straw hit the camel as I was focusing my camera on the large picture window of a home for another surprise gift. Adjusting my lens, I could clearly see the lady inside the house . . . focusing on me. I finished taking my photos and left as quickly as possible, calling my customer as soon as I reached home. "Your surprise is no longer a surprise," I told her. "Your mother saw me taking the photographs. Use your own judgment as to whether or not you wish to tell her about your gift."

My client called back later that morning. "I just finished telling my mother that I hired you to photograph her house for a drawing as my gift to her," she said. "I'm awfully glad you told me that she saw you and had looked concerned. There's been a rash of burglaries in her neighborhood and she nearly had a heart attack when she thought you might be 'casing the joint' for a robbery!"

I now require my customers to supply their own photographs.

- -

Pay Attention

Try to think ahead. Even though you're very involved in what you're doing, try to be aware of your surroundings and give some thought as to how it may appear to others.

17

REMBRANDT WAS NEVER WORRIED

s I became more skillful and my drawings improved, I tried to think of ways to make them more desirable.

I had no intention of going into time consuming oil paintings. (Rembrandt was never worried.) I wondered just how successful my drawings could be, in terms of marketability. If I were the buyer, I reasoned, I would be a lot more likely to purchase a nice drawing if it looked like MY house, MY face. So, rather than draw just any old house or face, hoping someone would come along and like it well enough to buy it, I decided to concentrate on finding the customer before I did the drawing.

That sounded reasonable. The only trouble with that idea was that I had to have a portfolio of sample drawings to display in order to secure the commission. If I handed over each finished piece to its new owner, what would I have left?

The pastel portraits, in spite of being sprayed with a fixative to prevent smearing, would not survive much handling. Besides, they were a little too large to fit handily into a carrying book. What to do?

Photograph the drawings. Great idea . . . 8" x 10" enlargements would do fine, and fit neatly into a notebook or album. My small X-15 camera, however, was not adequate for the job. A 35mm. model would do; but, unfortunately, it would be very expensive. I'd have to sell more than thirty portraits just to pay for the new camera.

Lucky for me, my nephew, David, the hockey coach, decided he wanted a motorized camera to photograph the players and the plays. He would sell me his manually operated 35mm. Minolta for a modest sum.

Of course, I did not know how to use it, so he explained. Unfortunately, he did so after 10:00 p.m., while I, with drooping eyelids, tried my best to pay attention. Naturally, I remembered very little the next morning. So, the following week I signed up for a Saturday photography class at our local high school.

We students introduced ourselves and stated what we hoped to get out of the class. Seated at the far end of the room, I began the round robin. (When will I ever learn?) "I bought this camera from my nephew. I finished my first roll of film and now I can't remember how to get the film out of the camera," I said honestly.

Each member of the class spoke his/her piece. It turned out that they all used photography in their jobs and just wanted to improve their techniques. And I had to open my big mouth in front of everyone and admit that I didn't even know how to get the film out of the camera. Ah well, so much for honesty.

What I hoped to learn was how to operate my new machine. As it was, I got more than I had bargained for. We were also required to develop our own film and work with the enlarger: burning, dodging, the whole bit.

A number of high points stand out in my mind about that class: such as the day I ran back and forth between the starting and the finish lines of the Western Springs Tower Trot. Four of our children and their friends, all long distance runners, competed in the 5K (Kilometer) and 10K races.

I photographed the runners at their mark, taking off, speeding away, and finally at the big FINISH. Several of them won medals. It was thrilling. And I had captured it all on film with my trusty 35mm.

Or had I? Encountering difficulty removing the film, I was appalled to open the back of the camera and find . . . nothing inside!

Without thinking, I whipped the lid shut and glanced furtively about me. I told myself, "Nobody saw that. If I can bluff it out, no one will ever know."

But that was hopelessly wishful thinking. They had all won their races. They were going to expect to see their pictures!

Revolting a thought though it was, I decided I had to admit my error in order to get them to pose for "another" photo . . . this time using film.

Each finally did pose, standing on one leg, medal 'round the neck, looking like a still frame from a moving picture. And they were all too polite to say what they must have been thinking. Actually, they didn't have the breath to comment; they were all rolling on the ground, laughing.

Things did improve. I almost always remembered to insert film from then on. Eventually I took photos of my embroidered fashions, as well.

All this took time. Because some of us learn more slowly than others, I thought it prudent to take the same class again. Halfway through the second class, I asked permission of the instructor to show him, and the rest of the group, my fashion slides for comment.

I intended to use these slides for talks, rather than cart all the clothing with me each time. (That is, if anyone ever asked me to give a talk again.) Of course, I hoped that he would be impressed with the quality of my work, both in fashion design and in photography. I had shown about a dozen slides when he interrupted, "Oh, hold it right there. That's perfect! I would love to have several copies of that slide for my collection."

I was surprised and thrilled. The slide was O.K., but I felt it was not even one of my best. "Oh, really?" I asked, trying to sound modest.

"Absolutely," he replied emphatically. "Right there, all rolled up into one perfectly horrible slide, are all the rules of things not to do. What a wonderful teaching tool!"

No one ever said things worth working for come easy. Needless to say, the vast improvement in my photographic abilities took a lot of work.

Interestingly, I found that many of the skills used in drawing portraits, landscapes and fashion illustrations were equally useful in composing effective photographs. Ultimately, I was asked to photograph the works of my fellow fiber artists, textile guild members and embroiderers, both for their personal portfolios and for jurying into competitive exhibits.

My most rigorous assignment was photographing a wedding . . . something I swore I would never do. The reason being, if I were to mess up in any way, two whole families would be ready to lynch me. A day came, however, when I felt obliged to honor a friend's request to photograph her wedding. Happily, my effort was successful.

My nicest compliment came quite unexpectedly from a young woman who saw the photos I had taken of our family. It was wintertime. "I never take a good picture. Never!" she stated simply.

"But you're lovely," I replied, noting her velvet brown eyes and the way her shining dark hair curled softly about the nape of her neck. "Why would you say that?"

"My mother carries current pictures of all my brothers and sisters in her wallet, but the one of me was taken when I was four." I could see that this was not simply a case of false modesty; she was serious.

"Call me on a sunny afternoon," I told her. "I'll take your picture, and you'll look beautiful."

She called a few weeks later when the weather had warmed and the sun was shining. I took 24 close-up portrait shots. She had them developed (I don't bother with that any more) and brought them back the following day.

"I lost 60 pounds this past year," she explained, "but I still think of myself as 'the fat lady'. That is, I did until I looked at these pictures."

"Gosh, I can't believe it." she said, with her eyes shining. "I really AM beautiful."

- -

Grow Into New Skills

Be honest when stating your level of skill. To be otherwise is not only non-productive, but also can be embarrassing.

Constantly seek to improve your skills. Ask for help and it will be given to you.

Use your skills in a cross-over manner. Abilities from one area can very often be transferred to another.

When you finally master a skill, be willing to share your ability with others, but temper your generosity with realism. Giving yourself away is not your goal.

18

NOTHING VENTURED, NOTHING GAINED

riday mornings, Diana England taught a class called New Directions for Women.

I don't know why I signed up for that particular class, other than it sounded interesting. On the first day, we took turns introducing ourselves and stating why we came.

With no prearranged thoughts as my turn came around, my mouth opened and seemed to operate on its own. "I grew up, saying: 'Yessir'; 'No, sir', and 'You know best, sir'. Lately, I've tried: 'No, please . . .' and 'No, because.' Although I don't want to make a career of it, I'd like to learn how to say just plain 'No!'"

For a moment, my ears couldn't believe what my bold mouth had said. All I could feel was a flush rushing up over my face. Suddenly, 18 fellow class members who were gathered around the huge library table, laughed and applauded.

Things progressed in the weeks that followed. We explored and shared ideas. Relieved to realize that we were not alone with many of our feelings, we encouraged each other to be brave and to learn to risk failure, or success, in order to TRY new ventures.

Was the class effective? I'll say it was! Midway through the quarter, each Friday morning I attended class and every Friday afternoon I applied for a new job. It didn't really matter whether I got these jobs or not. Perhaps I didn't seriously want them right then.

What was important was the fact that I was really starting to feel good about myself . . . confident and terrific. I had the need to test this newly found confidence by telling even a stranger how worth-while and wonderful I was.

It was, perhaps, this new found confidence that prompted me to inquire at the college placement office for a part-time student job. I was really enjoying my life drawing and fashion illustration classes when I discovered a request for a Creative Illustrator for a local manufacturer.

"Oh boy, oh boy, oh boy," I thought. "That's for me." I telephoned their office Friday afternoon. I answered, "Why, certainly," to all the fellow's questions and agreed to show up Monday afternoon with my portfolio.

I hung up the phone and hurriedly dialed my Fashion Illustration teacher, Bette Anderson. "Bette," I told her, "I have an interview to show my portfolio to a prospective employer Monday morning. Could you tell me over the phone how I can make one by then?" She did.

I researched the company's product, examined it at a local store and hurried home to draw people using it. My family graciously posed for me.

Armed with my drawings, a half dozen or so, with captions, I arrived for my appointment.

The owner was impressed with my drawing ability and with the obvious fact that I could think. The drawings were not only appropriate to the job at hand, but also were inventive.

I was elated with my luck at securing the interview and glad that he liked my sketches. (No way had I had time to prepare finished drawings.)

I was offered the job which was to begin the following week. Whoopee!

"By the way," I asked, as I was leaving, "you didn't mention what you were going to pay me."

"What do you expect?," he asked. (I expected that he would state a low figure; I would state something high; and then we would meet in the middle.)

So I said, "Well, five dollars an hour sounds good." (Minimum wage at that time was $2.50 to $2.75.)

"I'm sorry, that's too high. We can't afford you. Goodbye."

The next thing I knew I was on the outside, looking in. So much for negotiating.

The moral of the story is: when prospective employers ask what you think you should be paid, simply ask them what they have in mind. But make sure THEY talk first.

That was the bad news. The good news came the next day in the fashion illustration class when Bette asked, excitedly, "How did you make out? Tell us what happened. We're dying to hear."

I related my tale of woe and was considerably cheered when she said, "Never mind. It doesn't matter. It's not this job that counts. What's important is that you had the courage to apply for it and carry it through. My word, you've got guts! Three illustration classes, and you apply for a position! This experience is invaluable. I'm so proud of you!"

What a woman! What a teacher! Here I hadn't even gotten the job and she had me feeling like I'd won a medal!

- -

Be Ready for Success

Talk to people who have things in common with you. Realize you're not alone. Support and encourage one another to have the courage to risk failure or success.

Learn to feel good about yourself; you're a terrific person.

Do your homework so that when opportunity is yours, you'll be prepared for success.

When bargaining, if possible, let the other person state a price first.

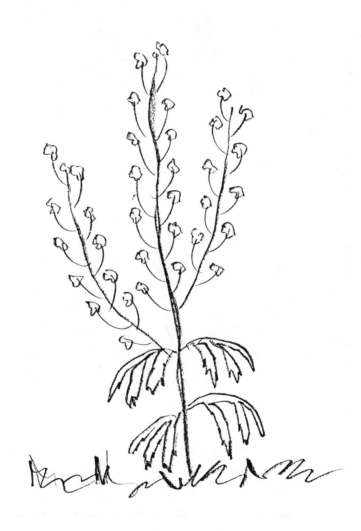

19

I MUST BE GOOD AT SOMETHING...BUT WHAT?

omehow, as time went by, the idea of earning money became more and more interesting.

The fiasco at the employment office taught me that having my last paid job listed as 17 years ago was not the greatest recommendation on my work record. What to do?

In spite of the fact that all the children were still at home, I managed to take two college classes fairly regularly. I then wondered if I could squeeze in a part-time job so that I could say, "Why certainly, I have been recently employed with so-and-so."

When I heard that a cashier was needed at the place where I took sewing lessons, I applied for the job and was accepted. My sewing skills came in handy in answering customers' questions. The work was all right.

It was recommended that sales personnel wear hand-sewn garments of stretch material to prove that they knew how to sew with the fabric. Being a pattern drafter and possessing three closets full of fabric before I got the job, I considered it sensible to draft my own patterns and use my own fabric. Somehow the wisdom of this escaped my employer, who suggested that I use my meager part-time wages to purchase patterns and fabric from her . . . or take myself elsewhere. I took myself elsewhere.

The next week, I heard that a local framemaker needed an assistant to block needlepoint and other stitchery. I called immediately and was granted an informal interview. I must have passed first muster because he gave me the final test, asking me to shake hands with him as hard as I could. I did . . . and got the job.

The mystery about the handshake test was soon dispelled as I pulled and tugged on the wispy margins of canvas threads that some bird brain of a stitcher had left 1/4" long instead of the regulation, and recommended, two inches. Nevertheless, things went well, as long as I worked for only two or three hours at a time.

Trouble came the day after I had devoted eight hours to blocking canvas: grasping, pulling and stretching heavy fabric into place. I was surprised to discover that I could not pick up a comb, a spoon, or anything else that required the grasping motion of thumb and forefinger!

The tendonitis only lasted for a week or two, but recurred the instant I tried doing the same work. Reluctantly, I left the framer. He was not terribly surprised, as several other assistants had run into the same problem. We were just a bunch of sissies, I guess.

Some work record I was building! I had stayed with each employer for only three months. This was going to require a little more thought.

I had already decided that staff nursing was out. So what else was available?

I soon realized that in answering any ad from the classified section of the newspapers, I would be competing for jobs with young men and women just emerging from college . . . 22 years old, ambitious, few home responsibilities, familiar with the latest techniques, probably attractive, and full of stamina. Yes, this was definitely going to require some thought.

I obviously needed an edge. With this competition, I certainly wasn't going to get a job just on my good looks and sparkling personality. Well, I hadn't been sitting on my thumbs for the past 20 years. I must be good at something! But what?

Perhaps I wasn't being objective enough. So, seeking some objective, knowledgeable and friendly advice, I asked a couple of my instructors with whom I had become friends, "In your opinion, what have you noticed that I can do as well as, or better than, anyone else, at which I can earn money?"

"Fashion design, pattern drafting, life drawing, clothing construction, and fashion illustration," they promptly replied. "Have you considered going into business for yourself?"

No, I hadn't. Not at all. I wanted to work for someone else who would pay me for doing something that I could do very well.

I investigated the position of fashion designer and found that fledgling fashion designers work long hours for very little pay just to get their feet in the door.

I also discovered that large department stores which use fashion illustration in their advertising, had most, or all, of their work done in New York. In addition to that, getting a job as fashion illustrator usually demanded the long arduous hours of any other full-time beginning professionals. My primary responsibility was still, for the time being, mother and homemaker.

Of course, I could, did, and still do construct clothing for myself and for the family. I decided, though, that I did not want to do it for others.

That left life drawing and pattern drafting. Now anyone who sews knows that a commercial pattern commonly requires some minor adjustment for each individual. When a person needs four or more major changes, however, it often becomes too complicated for the amateur sewer.

Therefore, I reasoned that my pattern drafting skills might prove to be marketable. I went 'round to all my local fabric stores to inform them of my new service. (These people knew me well, as I am a fabric addict.)

In the two years that followed it became apparent that custom pattern drafting was not too practical or profitable. Because requests for this service were so few, I decided to look for something else.

About the time that I began to pursue portrait drawing in earnest, I invested in a Bernina sewing machine. This was a costly device, which I was determined to make pay for itself. I learned, in the free lessons that were offered with its purchase, how to perform a number of tasks. The most difficult and frustrating of these was free-hand machine embroidery.

When drawing on paper, one pushes a pencil over the immovable paper. Whereas the method in free-hand machine embroidery is akin to pushing the paper (fabric) around under the stationary pencil (needle).

There are several requirements for accomplishing good free-hand machine embroidery. First, one must have a suitable machine. Second, one must use proper technique. And finally, one must be patient and extremely perseverant in order to achieve necessary control.

I may be slow, but I can persevere. After a great deal of practice, I acquired skill. It was a challenge. My control increased to the point where I could "draw" a person's portrait in machine embroidery and achieve a good likeness.

I was a fair calligrapher, too. After all, if I could stitch a portrait in machine embroidery, I could certainly stitch beautiful initials, letters of a foreign alphabet, flaming eagles, or sailing boats, as the job might require.

One thing led to another. I recognized what might be another opportunity. I went back to the fabric stores to inform them that I could now perform machine embroidered monogramming.

This, finally was something that worked out very well. The machine embroidery was a success.

- -

Keep Moving Toward Your Goal

Clarify your goals.
Identify steps which can lead to those goals.

Then START STEPPING! If you perceive obstacles, try to remove them or get around them. If you can't do either, find another route. Don't let anything stop you. **Keep moving!**

Stand back and re-evaluate your progress periodically. Know when to call it "quits" on a project.

Don't confuse an intermediate step with your final goal. Don't let yourself get sidetracked and bogged down in trivial matters. Keep your eyes on that final goal!

When looking for new ideas, consider all possibilities. Just because it isn't being done now, doesn't mean you can't do it.

When a new idea seems to be a success, see what you can do to make it even better.

20

WHERE WAS ALL THIS LEADING?

decided it was time to set a definite goal.

But I wasn't quite sure how to go about it.

I remember having an interview with the Dean of Admissions of the School of the Art Institute of Chicago. "Exactly what is it that you want to do? And where do you want to go?", she asked. Though it should not have done so, this perfectly valid, professional, businesslike question caught me by surprise.

Without stopping to think, I just blurted out, happily, "I have no idea, but I'm absolutely sure I'm on the right track."

"Oh, God, now I'm dead," I groaned inwardly. "As a dedicated student heading for a serious objective, I'm lucky enough to get this precious appointment for counseling and I'm babbling like an airhead."

Much to my astonishment, instead of telling me, "Beat it. Don't waste my time," she leaned back in her executive swivel chair and grinned delightedly. "Well, I don't know where you're going either. But I'm absolutely certain that you're going to make it."

We must have talked enthusiastically for over 20 minutes. I left with some class information, helpful advice and a great deal of encouragement.

Soon afterward, I requested an appointment with a career counselor at the College of DuPage. I needed sound guidance.

As it turned out, I never attended that first appointment. To set up the meeting, I spoke to a male counselor over the phone. He asked me a number of questions regarding my majors (fashion design and art), my grades (mostly A's), and my interests (many).

He was most enthusiastic about my possibilities until I mentioned that I was married and had several children. He then said drearily, "Well, there's not much point in our meeting, is there?"

"But why?", I asked.

"There's no future in either fashion design or art for you."

"What do you mean?", I asked again.

"Because those professions are already full up," he answered lamely.

NONSENSE!

Furious, I called the main office and asked to speak to another counselor . . . most definitely a woman, preferably married with children and most preferably with gray hair!

That's when I met Barb Schillin.

Because I knew that her time was limited, I was determined to make the most of what time there was. I organized samples of my work: portraits, house drawings, monogramming, and photographs of my fashion designs. I wrote down my interests in order of their importance and made a list of questions.

It was amazing. I entered her office with my thoughts in confusion and left knowing exactly what I wanted to do and how I might begin. We determined that I wanted to pursue a business of my own.

How she did it, I'm still not sure. I think she listened. She asked me questions; from my answers, she sifted out pertinent comments and asked me additional questions. She then told me what it sounded like I was saying.

All the information came from within me. She did not tell me what to do. Yet, somehow, in talking to Barb Schillin, my thoughts all shifted into order; I could, and did, state emphatically the direction that I wanted to take and what I wanted to do.

In the years that followed, I met with Barb twice more. The result was always the same. I entered her office uncertain of my direction and left with a solid plan.

- -

You Have A Right To A Sensible Explanation

When a professional person gives advice that is not clear to you, call a halt right then and there and ask for an explanation.

Sadly, many professionals deliberately intimidate their customers into accepting their (the professionals') advice without question.

DON'T DO IT! Have the self-confidence to insist on a clear explanation - or get rid of that person!

127

If a professional person (doctor, attorney, professor, mechanic, whoever) does not explain his ideas in CLEAR ENGLISH that you can understand, ask him to reword it.

If his explanation still makes no sense, ask him to draw you a picture - literally.

And, if he is <u>still</u> incapable of presenting his ideas in a way that makes sense, HIRE SOMEONE ELSE!

will grant audience

Forget it

PROFESSIONAL

FOR HIRE

All right

21

TAKING CONTROL LEADS TO STRENGTH
AND SELF-CONFIDENCE

hen I was a student nurse, I felt everyone outranked me: doctors, R.N.s, clergy, visitors, and patients. Everyone.

I'd pop to attention when just about anyone came into a room. A carryover from this experience made me feel for years that any professional person was doing me a great favor by responding to my needs.

Things have changed. Since I have become one, too, I now approach professional people with the expectation of mutual benefit.

I now insist upon knowing exactly what their service consists of; and, because of that, I feel more in control. If I wish to hire a person's services, I may do so. On the other hand, if his service, charge, or attitude doesn't suit me, I can (and will) take my business elsewhere. I no longer come as a beggar, hat in hand.

I find that this attitude of offering mutual benefit is carried over into relationships with my customers, also.

When a customer calls, requesting information about my services, I ask him questions about his purpose, as well. If I conclude that some other type of service would suit his needs better, I gladly refer him to someone else.

However, if I feel my skills can serve best, I say so. When that customer comes to my door, I do not feel that he is doing me a great favor. On the contrary, we meet with the expectation of mutual benefit.

I am delighted when people admire my drawing or stitching ability enough to pay me a fair price for it. I am happy to spend my valuable time, energy and skill responding to their requests.

Taking control, I set, not only my prices, but also the tone of my business relationships and the standards of my work.

I set my prices low enough to keep my services desirable, yet high enough to insure my continued enjoyment of my work.

I have come to realize that it is I who create the rapport between me and whoever comes through my door. In my business relationships, I set the tone that is comfortable for me: friendly and open, honest and straightforward, informal (but not familiar), attentive and professional.

I make a conscious effort to speak clearly and distinctly. I greet my customer at the door with a friendly smile, and, standing tall, extend my hand, look him straight in the eye and call him by his first name. "John, it's nice to see you. Come right in. Please call me Carol." I shake hands firmly, but with a care for arthritics.

I lead the way into my office, offer him a chair and walk 'round to sit behind my table (a large north window at my back). Colorful portfolios, representing my best work in each area of skill, are displayed before him.

I listen carefully to understand my customer's requests. Then, based on his needs, I offer suggestions.

Because of the laymen's inexperience in some areas, he or she may sometimes propose, or insist upon, a project that cannot be produced with quality.

When this happens, my professional standards and the confidence that I am the expert in my field make it necessary for me to refuse that particular job.

This confidence in my own judgment didn't appear overnight, like frost on a windowpane. It came gradually . . . the result of all the times I did my best.

- -

Build Little by Little

What a difference in the response of the people I deal with now, as opposed to ten years ago!

But to give them the benefit of the doubt, perhaps it is not THEY who have changed at all. It could be that they are merely giving me what I obviously expect: competence, fair dealing, courtesy, consideration, straightforwardness, honesty, excellent service, and respect.

I offer this to everyone I deal with. In turn, I expect, and will accept, nothing less. TRY IT!

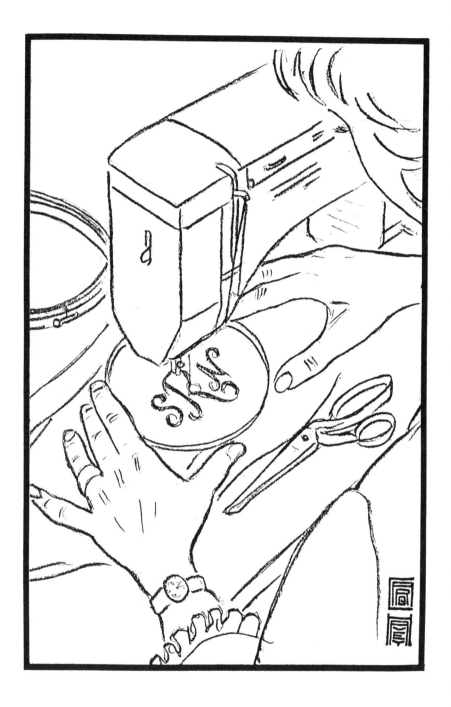

22

RISK = VALUABLE GROWTH

n a practical sense, there are limits to the amount of time I wish to spend executing fine work merely for my own enjoyment.

Growth is a constant cycle: research, experiment, variation, and expansion. If a project becomes boring, unsatisfactory, or impractical, I drop it.

On the other hand, if a project proves satisfactory, fresh, exciting, and desirable, I not only keep it, but constantly try to improve upon it.

There are several ways by which I market my skills. I sell the items or services, themselves. I sell information to individuals, as in color counseling. I also share information with groups in the form of lectures and workshops.

For the past several years, I have been writing, teaching, or lecturing on: personal color and fashion design; wardrobe coordination and makeup; color and embroidery; drawing for design; clothing embellishment; and balancing self, family, work, and home.

There is a time for everything: for investigating and learning, for experimenting and refining, for including or throwing away. But always a time for sharing.

It is only by risking new things that we can grow; only by growing that we are able to reach our greatest potential; and only in being the best that we can be that we can share our best selves with others.

- -

Learn To Fly

Time was that when a woman took a job, there she stayed for 30 years.

Things have changed as illustrated in a joke I heard the other day. When the personnel supervisor read on a woman's job application:
- "Company A - Manager, 1 year,
- Company B - Superintendent, 1 year,
- Corporation C - Vice-President, 1 year,"
he quipped, "What's the matter? Can't hold a job?"

It has been said that if you do exactly the same job for ten years, you don't have ten years of experience; you just have one year of experience - ten times!

Don't be content to stay in the same rut for the rest of your life. Risk a little - Grow a lot!

Stretch your wings - Learn to fly!

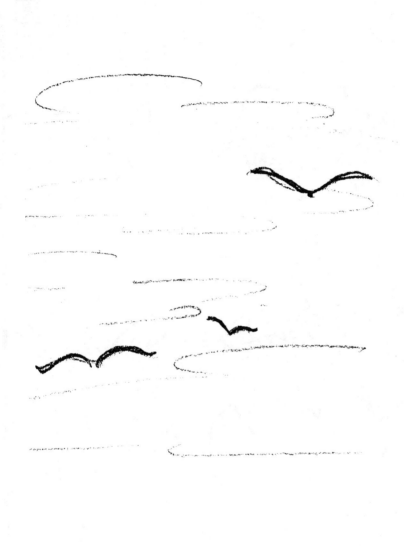

23

MY RAINBOW JOURNEY:
PROGRESS REPORT

ith each passing year, my skills and my customers increase.

Although I work primarily for individuals, some of my most exciting projects have been personal appearances doing on-the-spot monogramming at Neiman Marcus, I. Magnin, and Saks Fifth Avenue.

I have been in the business of free-hand machine embroidery since 1976 and I'm enjoying it more than ever.

I still do portraits of people and homes for framing. Meanwhile, I have discovered two other popular ways of presenting house drawings: pen and ink drawings which are reproduced to be used for Christmas cards or correspondence and outline drawings on canvas to be used for needlepoint.

Sometimes my portraits are of pets; difficult, but fun. Now and then, I am asked to create a coat-of-arms or design a business logo.

I use a flowing form of calligraphy for my machine embroidery. Occasionally, however, I incorporate a firmer style for addressing wedding invitations and for lettering certificates.

I have designed a variety of cards featuring scenes of local villages, and have had them printed and packaged for sale through local gift shops and historical societies.

In addition to these things, somewhere along the line, I was run over by a rainbow.

It is not surprising, when you consider that all forms of art overlap. And almost all of them involve color.

I became fascinated and completely enchanted with the whole phenomenon of color, in all of its aspects: chemical, physical, psychological, physiological, and, especially, visual.

Once I came to know the dynamic effects possible through the use of color, I was determined to build my skill. I experimented with harmonies and variations of the color wheel in fabric, creating quilts and clothing which I displayed both in fashion shows and fiber art exhibits.

When studying the optical illusions created by color, I began to comprehend the effect that color has on a person's appearance. I could understand the reason behind those illusions because of my background in many areas: art, nursing, portrait art, clothing design, and the study of color, itself.

By the time color counseling gained public recognition, it was a service I was already providing. This, combined with advice on fashion design, wardrobe coordination and makeup, has become one of my most rewarding occupations.

I take the most pleasure in it, knowing I give people valuable information they can use for a lifetime.

My most colorful works are my rainbow quilts: some using as many as 120 colors, arranged in prism-like order. I exhibit them on occasion, but for the most part, our family simply snuggles beneath them on chilly Chicago nights. (Rainbow quilts are much warmer than any old gray ones.)

Several years ago, I shared a very special thrill with several women of our parish, especially my friend, Kathy O'Neill. Kathy is a talented designer and stitcher, herself. We worked together to construct three liturgical wall hangings (three feet by ten feet) which I had designed. Seeing these, and a number of vestments which I had created, actually being used during services, as visual prayers for all to share, was a humbling and awesome honor.

Having these same wall hangings on display at the Cultural Arts Center in Chicago and at several national conventions was a privilege. Witnessing their use as part of the worship service was, indeed, the fulfillment of a prayer.

The more glamorous pieces of my work, of course, are clothing. As a fashion designer, I design each piece, draft the pattern, execute the hand or machine embroidery and/or Seminole piecework, then construct the garment.

My children, usually my oldest daughter, Julie, graciously model the pieces, while I do the fashion photography. This supplies prints for my portfolio and slides for jurying into exhibits or for color slide lectures.

Since relatively few fiber artists are skilled photographers, I am happy to photograph their work, also.

You may be wondering what a fiber artist is. She is one who works with fiber; spinning, dyeing, weaving, knitting, crocheting, tying, knotting, sewing, embroidering, stitching (of any sort), and fabric manipulation. The list is endless.

Creative, talented artist/craftswomen have formed specialty guilds all over the world. I have had the privilege to be an active member in two or more textile art and embroiderers' guilds since 1973.

Our textile guilds meet monthly or bimonthly for workshops and lectures; wherein we participate as students and sometimes as instructors. Each of the guilds has a biennial exhibit, in which we are all encouraged to enter several new and original pieces. To participate in such a group is not only a learning opportunity, but an energizing experience. We all stimulate each other's enthusiastic creativity.

This sort of atmosphere absolutely keeps me on my toes, and is just the kind of encouragement I need to keep experimenting and trying new things.

Each textile guild, just like each business women's group to which I belong, is an excellent support group.

- -

Get Ready!

By now you've already written a list of your short range and long range goals.

On a separate sheet of paper, write down where you started - and when.

Put the two papers together and mark your progress. Where have you come from? Where are you going? <u>Where are you now?</u>

Step back to get an overall view. How are you doing? Making any headway? Want to change some goals? Have you found out more information about them since you started traveling?

Constantly re-evaluate your situation. If you've found the paths to your goals blocked a few times, don't regard this as failure. Consider it useful experience that will better equip you to succeed in the future.

Don't be discouraged to realize that you have not yet progressed very far, either. This could be just the beginning of the exciting climb to your greatest potential! The beginning of your great adventure!

Are You Ready?

24

SUPPORT GROUPS EASE THE PRESSURE
AND NOURISH THE FLAME

veryone needs a support group!
If you don't belong to one, find one.
If you can't find one, start one. Members
may be family, friends, neighbors, fellow church
members, classmates, or people with a shared
interest, such as hobbies or business.

Being part of such a group keeps you in
touch with reality. When the problems and
pressures of your life get to be too much, it's
vital to be able to associate with people who
understand. It is essential to your well-being,
if only to assure you that you are not flying
through the twilight zone alone!

A support group not only helps to keep you
sane, but acts as a network to put you in touch
with the people and the information you seek as
your needs require. If you work in isolation,
without the benefit of personal or, at least,
telephone contacts, read, watch and listen. Use

the support offered to you through books like this, newspapers, magazines, and television.

Carol Kleiman, who has several weekly columns in the <u>Chicago Tribune</u>, writes about women at work. She and other writers, such as Joan Beck and Ellen Goodman, write columns which are syndicated around the country. They not only inspire women to do their best, but keep us informed of the most recent statistics, job opportunities, latest trends, and legal changes which will most affect our lives.

Sylvia Porter writes on money matters in her own magazine on personal finance.

These women, and those who write for <u>Working Woman, Ms., Savvy,</u> and other such magazines, are the best complement to, and can act as a substitute for, personal support groups.

Support groups are the best examples of women striving for excellence, not in competition, but within a spirit of cooperation!

Talk to your friends! Gone are the days when all we were politely permitted to speak about were zinnias and the weather!

Seek not only your own personal growth and development, but share your progress with other women - that they, too, will be encouraged to strive for excellence and achievement!

Don't keep the fire of your success to yourself - pass it on!

PART III
Roles We Play

25

YOU CAN'T GIVE WHAT YOU DON'T HAVE

t's only after building strength, self-confidence and satisfaction with your life that you are able to share these things with others.

We support each other through our many and varied roles which change throughout the years.

What are some of the roles you play? Person, child of God, daughter, sister, friend, wife, mother, homemaker, hobbyist, worker, professional, entrepreneur, widow, grandmother? These are just some of many possibilities.

The goal of a well-balanced life is to juggle many of these roles at the same time, without destroying the others. Of course, we all work on a priority basis. Just as the squeaky wheel "gets the grease"; so, too, does the loving role relationship in direst need get the attention first.

Although we often handle many roles simultaneously, successfully and smoothly, there are times when we have to drop everything else in order to give our complete attention to the relationship with the most urgent need. It is important, however, that we remember that balance in our lives ultimately depends upon the fact that all three areas of our spirit (in God, in each other, and in ourselves) require our attention.

To deny God is to be an atheist. To deny others is to be an egotist. Yet, to deny yourself is to be a doormat. None of these states is desirable or meritorious.

Harmony exists only through balance. Only by giving loving attention to God, others, and ourselves, can we achieve a state of harmony wherein we are capable of making the most of the gifts that God has given us.

No two people are alike; nor do we have the same abilities. It is not what we have that matters most. It is what we make of it that counts.

Each day is an opportunity to begin anew and to show our respect and appreciation to God for the talents given us by making the most of those gifts and sharing them with each other.

It begins with you!

You can't give what you don't have.

26

CHILD OF GOD

elp me each day to choose a right path.

Once I have made my choice, please help me to do my best, with good cheer and enthusiasm, to complete the task successfully.

Once I have done my part to the best of my ability, help me to accept the outcome. More than that, help me to willingly embrace the outcome knowing that you love me and know what is best for me.

Amen.

FRIEND:
YOU HAVE TO BE ONE

ancy was my best friend.

She was almost five years old and I was three. She lived two doors away.

I spent countless happy hours sitting in Nancy's kitchen, petting her dog Buster and watching her grandmother make wonderful things like strudel, noodles and fantastic sugar-covered pastries with German names I couldn't pronounce.

Although Nancy was two years older than I, and my sister, Ann, was six months older still, you could say the three of us were best friends. I was perfectly happy.

Years went by and Ann started high school. She no longer had time for Nancy and me, except perhaps during summer vacation. She always had something else to do: new friends, activities and dating.

That broke up our happy threesome, but Nancy and I still had fun. I was content.

That next fall, my mother totally surprised me with the suggestion that I had better start making some new friends. Nancy was due to go to high school the following year and would likely do as Ann had done. She would probably get so busy with new things, that she would no longer have time for me.

Of course, I found that hard to believe.

On the other hand, it could get pretty lonesome.

What if Mom was right? Perhaps I had better start making some new friends; except, I didn't know how.

I looked around my fifth grade class and decided I'd like to be friends with Diane. Diane sparkled. Generous, warm and friendly, Diane was always laughing and in good spirits. It was great fun to be around Diane.

Little by little we became good friends. We still are. It was easy for Diane. Hard for me.

I wanted so much to learn how to make friends like she did. I even got a book from the library: How To Win Friends and Influence People, by Dale Carnegie. He suggested that if you are really self-conscious about meeting people, talk to them about themselves. The idea being that they will be so interested in the subject, they won't notice nervousness on your part. Then, once the conversation gets going, you just won't be nervous any more.

I heartily recommend the book because I tried it and it definitely helped. Lucky for me, because Mom was right. Nancy went off to new adventures of her own and did not have time to look back.

I learned one of my first big lessons from this: the world is not going to beat a path to your door. If you want something, friends or whatever, you'll have to go out and find it, yourself.

Once we got into high school, Diane and I met a great bunch of girls with whom we shared many interests. We formed a club and called ourselves the Shoshones. In a school like Calumet (which is an Indian name, meaning peace pipe), many of the school clubs had Indian names: Apaches, Tomahawks, Sioux, etc.

The Shoshones began meeting on the third Friday of the month in 1950 and we've been doing it pretty much the same ever since. There may be as many as twelve of us, or as few as three or four. It's more or less a standing date.

A Hollywood comedian once quipped, "We were so poor . . ." (How poor were you?) "We were so poor that we couldn't even afford an analyst; we had to make do with old friends!"

You know, he's right. We joke that we would have gone stir crazy years ago, if it were not for our "homemade psychotherapy group." We tried playing cards once, but decided we really didn't have time for that. We still don't; there is always too much to discuss.

It's a very peculiar phenomenon. No matter how terrible an event can be during the month, once you can bring yourself to speak of it out loud (and that may take more than a month, sometimes) it doesn't seem so bad. Even the most awful things shrink, somewhat, once you can talk about them. Furthermore, if you can get to the point where you can just throw up your hands and laugh about it, things come back into

161

perspective again, so that, once more, you can see that all is not lost.

We often help each other with information, too. On the other hand, sometimes all we can do is listen, and perhaps say, "Oh, how rotten! And then what did you do?" This gives the person an opportunity to explain how she managed to cope.

I have learned a great deal from my friends at club meetings. We are survivors. Our lives are not without problems. If those problems don't get solved one way; we will find another way.

Old friends are special treasures. You don't have to prove anything to old friends. Even when you make a mess of things, they don't throw you away.

The most important thing I have learned, however, is that friendship is reciprocal. You can't go out and just look for a friend; all you can do is BE one.

YOUNG WOMAN:
DON'T WAIT FOR THE WORLD TO CHANGE

omen's lives are changing rapidly in this country.

And what comes next?

No longer can we plan that our lives will be like those of our mothers. They won't. They can't; it's too late for that. There have been too many changes in lifestyles, laws, the work force, and in demographics for us to predict just what shape our lives will take.

What can I tell you, my young adult daughter, but to follow my example in some things and avoid my mistakes in others.

Only education can empower you with the opportunity to choose your life's path. Therefore, work hard to put yourself through college in order to learn a marketable skill by which you can earn a good living, hopefully, doing something that you enjoy.

Study hard to earn good grades, so that, in today's keen competition, you will be chosen for the best paying job.

Play hard to keep physically fit. You only have one body. When it's gone, you won't be able to purchase another.

Pray always. Keep in touch with God, your best friend.

Cultivate a sense of humor; you will need it.

Firmly establish a career in your early and mid-twenties; and live on your own, independently, at least for a while.

In your mid-to-late twenties, marry your best friend, someone with whom you want to spend the rest of your life.

Have as many children as you and your husband want to have and can care for. It's no one else's business. Use maternity leaves or leaves of absence until you can get competent, trusted day care to help you.

Then work temporarily, or part-time, or full-time. Consider what your energy can handle, what your profession requires and what opportunities you can find or create. When the children are older, you will once again need employment for income. As competition keeps increasing, it is important to retain your employability.

Stay insured and save income for your retirement. Then learn how to invest that income to make your money work for you to earn more.

Nurture interesting, worth-while, educational, and, better yet, profitable hobbies in which you can engage wholeheartedly when you retire from your main professional job.

So much for ideal advice. Do things always work out according to plan? Hardly ever. Is that the way I did it? No. Does it allow for unforeseen developments? No, again.

It's just a plan, better than most . . . and certainly better than none at all. After all, if you don't even know where you are heading, how can you possibly hope to get there?

What if you are already married or have children? You are committed to responsibilities that you cannot, and would not, abandon in order to follow the career path you omitted earlier. Maybe it's too late to opt for a formal career. What can you do now?

There's no plan that's perfect for everyone. You must begin from the place where you are right now. If you think you don't have time, try reorganizing your activities and setting priorities. You can make your life better than it is by taking stock of your assets, making your own plan and pursuing it.

The secret is, don't wait for the world to change or for some other person to make you a gift of your heart's desire. Zero in on what it is that you really want and go after it yourself because no one is going to do it for you.

Of course, there will be some things over which you have no control, in which case, you do the best you can. But, you don't quit. You never quit doing your best to make the most of your life!

29

TODAY'S WOMAN:
MY GRANDMOTHER NEVER DID THAT

omen's attitudes have mightily changed for a great many very good reasons.

To persons who rarely recognize the need for change, that may seem strange. "My grandmother and my mother never did that." they will object. "Why should I?"

For starters, our grandmothers did not have to worry much about life after 40; they were usually dead by then. Of course, our own mothers lived longer. When they reached 40-55 and felt bad, sad, mad, afraid, alone, nervous, and run down, a helpless shrug would intimate, "It must be the CHANGE," and blame it all on hormones.

Latest reports tell us American women can now look forward to living more than 80 years. It does not take a genius to figure out that a 30 year old mother, whose children are in grammar school, will probably be about 52 when those children are ready to graduate; and, according to plan, leave home. With divorce and widow-hood an all-too-common fact of life, that leaves her ready for 30 years of . . . what?

The most recent statistics reveal several dismal facts:

1. 1983 - per capita income, male = $18,109
2. 1983 - per capita income, female = $8,780
3. 1984 - average widow's social security benefit = $6,000
4. 1984 - designated poverty level = $5,278

As parents, we do not treat our children as little tots for 20 years, then expect them to behave as capable adults on their twenty-first birthday. Neither is it reasonable to expect a woman, who has worked in the seclusion of her own home for 30 years, to step into the role of independent "woman of the world" on the day that her last child, and possibly her husband, leaves home. She, too, must prepare for her new role gradually.

A woman may remember such platitudes as, "All good things come to her who waits." Whereas, it is far more likely that she who waits too long will gather flies, dust, moss, and a lot of other things too fierce to mention. A person can grow old just sitting around waiting. She must make things happen, herself.

While fate and the actions of other people are beyond our control, we <u>can</u> take charge of our own actions. Aware of this fact, therefore, the intelligent, mature woman will look ahead and start planning for her own future today.

30

WIFE:
CHOOSING A HUSBAND

ne of the most important decisions you will ever make is choosing your husband.

I hope you have the good sense to marry your best friend. The person with whom you want to spend the rest of your life because you like each other best of all and have fun together.

Be loyal to him. You have chosen each other for always. Know that you each come first with the other. Everyone else is second: parents, children and friends. Everyone!

Pay attention to him. When he's telling a story or a joke to others, look at him. Be ready to laugh and enjoy it as if it were the first time you had heard it.

Appreciate him. Seek the opportunity to honestly praise him or his activities, especially in the presence of others.

Be courteous. Respect each other's privacy, opinions, feelings, and dignity.

Render thoughtful, small courtesies to each other frequently. Pour his coffee. (Men: pour her wine. Send her flowers.) Bring him flowers. Lay out his pajamas. (Hold her coat.) Little things for no special reason other than to say, "I think you're swell; and I love you."

Touch each other. Kiss, hug, hold hands, caress. Touch each other passing through the hall. Wink at each other from across the room.

Worship together regularly with the children.

Learn from each other and about each other. No one stands still in life. We either shrink or continue to grow. Share and grow with each other.

Arrange for some regular alone-time together. Try to have a date at least once a week, away from the children, even if it is only to share a pizza or a walk in the park. Arrange it so that you won't be interrupted by the children or the telephone.

Most importantly of all, communicate, and keep communicating. Everyone has feelings; you are entitled to them. It is your responsibility to speak up and share those feelings with your husband. In order to love you, he must know you. In order to know you, he must understand you. Since he is not a mind reader, how is he going to understand you if you don't tell him how you feel? Tell him. And, be ready to listen to his feelings, as well.

Finally, HAVE FUN. Sometimes your sense of humor is all you have. Hang onto it. Enjoy each other.

31

MOTHER:
HOW TO REAR SUCCESSFUL CHILDREN
. . . SUCCESSFULLY

or starters, you never assume every
child will be a big success.

Such a smug attitude tempts fate.

Even if your children are big successes,
wouldn't it be egotistical to assume that you were
responsible for it all? Rather, you do what you
can, one day at a time, and hope for the best.
Then, after a certain point, their success or
failure is theirs, not yours.

I told my family that I wanted to share ideas
about rearing children. I asked them, "What
particular suggestions do you think have worked
out fairly well for us?" Their responses are
included in the following thoughts.

Be consistent. Do not say something unless
you mean it. Once you say it, stick by your
decision. Then you can be trusted. (Of course,
be open to reason.)

Be fair to all. What you do for one, be prepared to do for all. If the boys take turns washing clothes and doing dishes, let the girls take turns hauling out the trash and stripping woodwork. Be fair with privileges, too.

Worship together . . . in their presence. Integrity and values are taught by example, not with words. Don't be discouraged if you do not feel spiritually uplifted each time you go to worship, either. I think that is expecting too much. Just keep plugging along, doing what you know or think is the right thing to do. The benefit is the strength that comes when you need it most.

Give the children responsibility for jobs, little by little, THEN LET THEM DO THEM. Of course, it is more of a hassle this way for you, but how else are they ever going to learn?

Do not be afraid to talk about money in their presence. Explain the situation. They are not morons; neither are they mind readers. How can they be expected to cooperate, if they do not know what is going on?

Talk to your children as if they were people. They are.

You deserve respect. Respect your children's feelings and dignity, too. (Especially in the presence of others.)

Do not be afraid to set boundaries. Your children keep stretching, reaching, pushing to find limits, to see how far they can go.

Do not be afraid to admit that you do not know everything. The task of parenting does not come with a set of blueprints. You learn the skill on the job. In the meantime, however, since you have been around longer than your children, they will just have to trust your best judgment on some things. You may not be right, but you will just have to keep doing the best that you can.

Remember, what may be of great interest and importance to you, truly may be of no interest or importance to your children. Of course, some things need to be done, but try to see their point of view, too.

If your children are knowledgeable about a subject, ask them to teach you . . . and pay attention. You could learn something.

Ask your children how they are doing, with specific questions . . . and LISTEN to their answers. Respond with interested questions and remarks.

Let your children earn their own spending money and college tuition. They will respect and appreciate it.

Reserve "no" for necessary occasions. Say "yes" as often as you can.

Call family meetings periodically.
- All must attend.
- Ask children to make a list of chores.
- How do they want to distribute them?
- Does anyone have any gripes?
  . Each may speak, in turn, without being interrupted.
  . They must stick to the point.
  . They cannot drag out old history.
  . Each, in turn, may have a rebuttal.
  . They may not raise their voices.
  . They speak at the family meeting, or hold their peace afterward.

Only when the children take turns doing chores, do they appreciate the time and effort that is required to accomplish them.

Be on the lookout for opportunities to praise a job well done. Make use of these opportunities. Be honest.

Touch each other: hug, tickle, hold hands, kiss, massage a sore neck.

As a "life/career counselor", talk quietly, and as often as the opportunity presents itself without distraction. Talk about what they want to do with their lives.

- What are their talents?
- What do they like to do?
- Ask them short questions to get them thinking about this. Remember, their lives, not yours, are being planned.
- Of course, you could cut out articles from current publications which are pertinent to the topic in order to help them stay informed of the latest business opportunities.
- Discuss their unique personality traits and how these traits might serve as real assets in certain jobs.

Show the same courtesy to your children that you want them to show you. Yet, do not "let the tail wag the dog." It is your house and you are the parent.

Try to be patient with harmless peer pressure. It is a very strong force and it keeps changing. For example: if "everybody" wears rainbow suspenders . . . what is the harm? Save your vetoes for the time when "everybody" drinks alcohol at parties, smokes pot, or does other things too fierce to mention.

Do not tell your children that they are rotten, evil and wicked. DO stress that they are much too precious and worthwhile to be blown away on such senseless and destructive activities.

Have fun together as often as possible. Ask your children to join you in fun things. And, when they invite you, if at all possible, stop what you are doing and join in. If you keep refusing, they will soon stop asking. And the day will come when you would give anything to be included.

Though it requires constant refocusing, respect your children as persons in their own right, as men and women entitled to their own opinions, decisions, etc., just as you are.

Enjoy them for as long as you have them at home; but, when they are ready to move out and be on their own, let them go.

32

MOTHERS AND CHILDREN:
LET US ENJOY EACH OTHER

ur actions today influence our relationships for many tomorrows.

The fun we started long ago continues.

One night, several years ago, I asked the boys at the supper table, "What's the important look in high school these days?"

The answer was instant and unanimous, "Anonymity!"

While I realize that there is no one in the world so vulnerably dignified as a high school freshman boy, I know that young girls are also painfully conscious of calling undue attention to themselves.

When Julie was about eight, she asked one Sunday, "Mom, could we do that fun stuff today that just you and I do?"

"What's that, Jule?" I asked.

"Streetwalking!" she replied with a grin.

Bill hadn't been paying much attention up until this point, but then his eyes flew open. He sat up straight. Alert, he asked cautiously, "What do you mean, Julie?"

"You know, when Mom and I walk along the street and look in all the windows, but we don't really buy anything."

Exasperated, but relieved, I explained, "Julie, that's window shopping, not street walking. There's a difference!"

With five younger brothers at home, window shopping was a nice way for Julie and me to have some alone time together.

"Only two things, Mom," she pleaded with me one day on our way to the train station, "Could you please not skip? And could you try to keep your singing down when people get close enough to hear?" (A person might think they didn't let me out much.) However, out of respect for Julie's dignity, I tried to keep my cabin-fever-release jubilation down to a minimum . . . and I only skipped when she wasn't looking.

Julie is married now. We still look forward to an occasional afternoon when we get together and enjoy each other's company. She works odd shifts in the intensive care unit at the medical center, so our outings are often impromptu.

Our last luncheon together was at Marshall Field's 7th Floor Tower Restaurant at Water Tower Place along Chicago's Magnificent Mile on Michigan Avenue. Enjoying our day immensely, I ordered spinach salad and instructed the waitress solemnly, "No matter how much I plead or beg after our salad . . . do NOT bring me any of your chocolate mint pie!"

Unflappably professional, she smiled and went to get our order. When she returned, I asked politely, "May I have some coffee when it's convenient for you, please?"

"No," she replied, just as soberly as I, then turned and walked away.

I was flabbergasted and must have looked it. My back was turned, but Julie could see the waitress grinning broadly enough to eat a banana sideways as she made her way to the coffee pot. By the time our lady returned, Julie was nearly falling out of her chair laughing. "You should have seen the expression on my Mom's face when you walked away!" she gasped.

Of course, I got my coffee. When lunch was over, our funny waitress bent with a flourish and whispered, "These are a gift from me to you." She presented me with three luscious fudge mint chocolates in their individual little fluted paper cups resting on a paper lace doily on Marshall Field's finest china.

Fun times, started long ago with my children, continue. I was taught how to have fun by my mother before me.

Born in St. Louis, Missourri, Mom spent many an evening at the famous outdoor St. Louis Municipal Opera, listening to Nelson Eddy and Jeanette MacDonald. Although Mom will be 89 this year, she has a great memory. She and my sister, Ann (the barbershop singer), are the only two people I know who remember every little ditty and rhyme they've ever heard and break into song at the drop of a spoon, or hat, or anything else.

Now, Ann gets her singing talent from our Dad, I guess, who sang bass in a barbershop quartet. Mom, on the other hand, never claimed to be a singer. Since she suffered a whip lash in an auto accident about 15 years ago, hurting her throat, her voice breaks frequently.

Anyway, Mom left her St. Petersburg home last year to spend the summer with us, and as usual, helped me by doing most of the cooking. Cooking is not my best skill. I had struggled with a recipe for about an hour, when I finally called to Mom, "I give up. This whole thing is a mystery to me!"

She grabbed me by both shoulders, looked me straight in the eye, and cracked into song, "Aaaah, sweet mystery of life, at last I've found you. Ooooh, at last I know the secret of it all!"

O heck! With the fun of Mom's company, who cares about cooking, anyway?

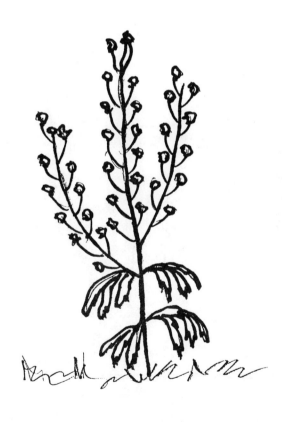

33

HAPPY PERSON:
RELISH PRECIOUS MOMENTS,
THEY MAY NEVER COME AGAIN

irst you learn how to stay alive.

Then you learn how to laugh to make it worthwhile.

My friend, Marcia, is an expert.

Skinny as a reed all through high school, gaining weight after having several children came as a real surprise to Marcia. She tried dieting, but quit in disgust. "I drank two cans of that darn chocolate diet stuff with my lunch all last month and gained five pounds!"

We cracked up with laughter, and choked out, "Marc, you're supposed to drink it instead of, not in addition to, lunch." Marcia's blank face turned color as she realized her mistake. She slapped her knee and laughed more than anyone, enjoying the joke she had unwittingly played upon herself. The next time she sought to lose weight, she included exercise.

I exercised regularly, myself, at that time with Gloria on T.V. About a week prior to the birth of our twins, John and Mary, I really counted on that morning stretch to keep my back limber enough to get through the day.

Gloria started out each session by saying, "Take your tape measure, and write down your vital statistics before we begin." After dutifully taking my statistics, all I could do was laugh or cry. I called Marcia, instead.

I omitted the courteous formality of identifying myself, blurting out, "O, Marc, have I got a figure problem! I just took my measurements and I'm 44-44-44!"

Obviously, my name wasn't necessary. She didn't know that many people with that kind of shape. We laughed till we cried.

Marcia's a real comfort to talk to.

A year and a half later, I remember another one of our phone conversations. "Hi," she said, "I just called to say, 'Hello.'"

"Could you hold on just a minute?" I asked. "People are just leaving."

"Goodbye, honey. Have a good day at work. Call me if you get time," I waved to Bill.

"Julie, hold Chris's hand crossing 99th Street," I warned the oldest who was in second grade.

"Mark, be sure your boots come home with you this time; preferably on your feet. No, don't worry about the Great Dane across the alley. I know he's big; but the fence is bigger," I soothed.

"No, Dan, you can't play out in the yard today. I killed thousands of bees out there yesterday. But there are still a lot of live ones left . . . and they're very upset," I cautioned.

"John, what have you done to your sister!?" I screeched.

"Mary, get out of that Malt-O-Meal!" I ordered.

"Kevin, hush, here's your bottle. There now," I crooned.

"I'm back, Marc. What did you say? What are you doing?"

"O, I'm playing with the baby; we're making faces at each other. He's so funny."

"Good grief," I thought. "Who has time to PLAY with the baby?"

That's when I remembered that this was Marcia's third son. Her first son died of a congenital heart condition when he was two and a half years old.

Marcia reminded me of something very important. Take time to relish precious moments when they occur; they may never come again.

34

SINGLE MOTHER/WORKER:
LEAVING THE MAGIC KINGDOM

here's one situation I have not yet mentioned . . . because it is one of the most difficult: that of the single mother/worker.

When a woman has more jobs than her energy and time can accommodate, she eliminates some, then evaluates what is left, in order to get her priorities straight as quickly as possible.

Facts she knows for certain:
- My children exist here and now.
- My husband (for all practical purposes) does not exist.
- I love my children completely. Otherwise, considering the easy availability of contraception, abortion, and adoption, I would not have them.
- Since my children are young, and incapable of caring for themselves, they depend upon me totally.
- My children cannot wait. Thus, I do not have the luxury of extra time at my disposal; my children need me now.

- Therefore, if I want to insure their welfare, I must gear myself for one of the most important and challenging tasks of my life: supporting my children by myself.

This very situation is reminiscent of the road sign outside the park of Disney World in Florida: "You are now leaving the Magic Kingdom" . . . where fairy tales come true and wishing will make it so; where fairy godmothers, elves, and enchanted princes appear from nowhere to make right your broken dreams. On the contrary, this is the real world. The fact that often-times it is not fair, easy, or fun has no bearing on the matter.

As for the roles a woman plays, my role right now is single mother/worker. Forget person/wife/homemaker. All take a back seat to the persons I care about even more than I care about myself: my children. Their welfare, even their lives, depend entirely upon my ability to provide for them. That will probably mean that my job is our lifeline. I will not have the luxury of staying home, myself, with my little ones; I must be employed. Furthermore, the expense of hiring a reliable sitter will be an additional, but vital, strain on the budget.

All these things are strong motives for me to pursue the very best paying job that I can possibly secure. Therefore, if improving myself, adding to my education, and developing my skills will result in bettering my position, then this must be my goal. I have the best reasons in the world to reach my greatest potential: my children and myself.

35

DAUGHTER:
HONOR THY FATHER AND MOTHER

s our parents get older, I wonder who will take care of them?

This is certainly a serious concern for many of us. Yet, who is to tell another adult person what she must, or must not, do? All of our circumstances differ. We all have our own problems and limitations. For me to spell out the moral obligations of another would be presumptuous, at best.

The best advice I can give is to treat your parents as you would like to be treated . . . and do the best you can.

The behavior of all of us is interrelated. Although your children may not speak of it aloud, they observe you and learn from your attitudes, as well as from your actions. Parents, on the other hand, are more set in their ways. Some have the kind of personality that drives you crazy. Others are a joy, a welcome support and a comfort. While you cannot control the actions of your parents, you can control your own.

For many years, my mother, who is now in her late 80's, has kept her own small home in Florida and has spent her summers, May-October, with our family. It has been a good relationship.

How can I account for such harmony?

It is certainly not that I am headed for sainthood. It has more to do with my mother's own attitude and actions. One time, I asked her about it.

Every morning and every night, she prays that she might be able to be of service to others.

Both she and my husband's mother (our fathers died long ago) offer advice only when I request it, even after all these years, and complain about aches and pains only when asked.

Neither one criticizes me. In fact, I have never heard either of them put anyone down. On the contrary, they rarely miss an opportunity to praise me or someone else on a job well done, often in the presence of others.

I will try to remember our parents' good example as our own children marry and have families of their own. I hope I will be as welcome with our children as our mothers are with us.

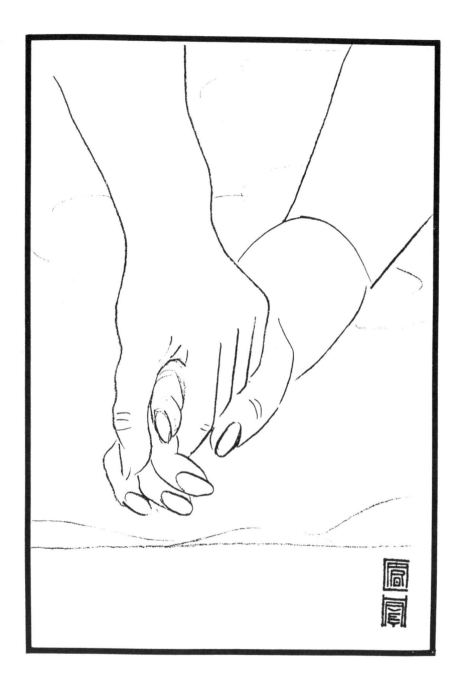

36

THE SINGULAR WOMAN:
SINGLE, DIVORCED, WIDOWED

hether you are single, divorced or widowed, as a woman on your own, it is more important than ever to be independently strong in these areas:
- psychological
- emotional
- financial.

The single woman who is a member of a religious community shares the unique benefit of a collective strength.

Additionally, her community provides spiritual support and fulfills the very basic human need for companionship.

Because God made us social beings, we have an instinctive need to care for, and to share our lives with, others.

You are lucky if you have loving parents, brothers, sisters and perhaps extended family, close by. Some of us, however, are not so fortunate. Immediate, and other, family members either don't exist, have died, or live so far away that contact is rare.

Furthermore, even though our culture is couple oriented, not all of us are destined for a romantic partnership.

Still, **we all need companionship.**

Our world is full of people yearning for a friendly word and for someone to notice them.

Young and old, there are those who need your personal friendship.

For **your** benefit, as well as theirs, don't be stingy. Share yourself.

Even though you may be happily married now, it may not last forever. This is not meant to alarm you, but simply to remind you that divorce occurs frequently and we all die sooner or later, men usually at a younger age than women.

Do this for yourself, right now:

Look over this year's calendar. Then look back on last year's.

How many times during any month did you and your husband have an engagement with friends? Think about the time when you first met them. Were these people originally your husband's friends or his business contacts?

Count up the occasions.

All the people with whom you spent your time . . . were they your husband's friends to begin with? Don't misunderstand. The fact that they met him first does not necessarily make them any less friendly. Yet, if circumstances were to change, and there would be only you, would you have that much in common with them anymore?

How often have you met a bewildered widow or divorcee, months after the loss of her husband, who hurtfully cries, "No one includes me any more. They want nothing to do with me." Sadly, this happens often, when the original contact, the husband, is gone.

If most of your social partners are business acquaintances and their wives, where would that leave you, if your husband were no longer here?

It would leave you home alone, wondering where everybody went; that's where.

Do not allow yourself to drift inadvertently into this lonely position. Look around. Make yourself aware of your circle of friends. Build your own network. Look for family, church members, neighbors, old friends, former classmates, new classmates, interest groups, and women's clubs.

It is all right for husband and wife to lean on each other in time of need, but each of us has to be ready to stand alone when necessary.

Timing is extremely important. God forbid anything should cause the loss of your husband. If that loss does come to pass, though, and you have had a happy marriage, grief and sadness would be inevitable. Terrible, but there it is.

Many other side effects often accompany the loss of one's spouse, however, that you can do something about. Do not wait until you are forced into action. Invest your efforts toward building a future for yourself, not just financially . . . but emotionally, psychologically, intellectually, and physically.

It comes down to this: are you content to merely drift along with the current, hoping for the best? Or, are you willing to invest your own efforts to create a positive future for yourself?

PART IV
Working

37

WORKER:
NO ONE GETS PAID FOR DOING NOTHING

ear God: Let me and the product of my work be useful to others. This is my prayer.
Amen.

It is also the prayer of most mature, intelligent men and women. We do for each other. I help you; you help me. No one person can do everything.

Long ago, and in some areas of the world even now, people bartered for goods and services. Since that is inconvenient in most places, now we simply use money as our common medium of exchange. However, our reasons for working remain the same:

- We want to serve a useful purpose.
- We desire a challenge.
- We want to create or build something beautiful, wonderful, or at least useful.
- We want to use our many capabilities to the fullest.

- We want our efforts to be acknowledged, appreciated and rewarded.
- We want some assurance that efforts during our days of strength will serve to support us when we tire.

I am willing and eager to earn my way. No one gets paid for doing nothing. If I wish to be able to purchase the goods and services of others later on, I must, in turn, render goods and services of equal value now. Fair is fair.

Therefore, I cannot afford to give away or squander my labor now, during the days of my strength. I would be a fool if I truly expected to live forever with unbounded vigor and energy. I realize that I am going to grow older, just like everybody else. When I do, it will be mighty nice to know that I do not have to work eight to sixteen hours a day just to provide food, shelter and clothing for myself.

It would be even better if I could afford to travel a little with my spouse; or be benevolent, and give gifts, now and then, to my children or grandchildren when I would be of a mind to do so.

It would be wonderful to wake each morning filled with enthusiasm, eager to begin my day's work, whatever it might be; loving the work that I do and knowing it will be appreciated. Best of all, would be the assurance that these very efforts of mine would be earning the means to accomplish other things that I want to do.

Does that not sound like heaven on earth? You can work on creating just this situation, if you really want to. It requires that you decide several things:
- What do you want? To travel, to write,

to paint, to hunt seashells? What?
- What is needed to bring this about?
  More education? Money? What?
- What can you do to make it happen?
- Where would you begin?
- What are your skills? Your interests?
  Your talents? Your assets?
- What can you do as well as, or better
  than, anybody else?
- Do you enjoy doing it?
- Is there a market for it?
- Can you get paid for it?

Suppose your present situation poses a problem. For instance, you may already have a job, but dislike it. Try changing jobs. If you cannot change jobs, try your best to enjoy it. You will have fewer ulcers.

However, if you have a necessary job that you enjoy, like taking care of your own small children, for which you receive no income, investigate every possible way you can think of to acquire money, while, at the same time, attending to that very necessary job.

It is never too late to succeed. Since very few of us are in the position we most desire, we must rise above our circumstances. We must decide first what we want and how we can get it, then we must start **doing something** about it.

38

WOMAN'S WORK IS NEVER DONE:
AND IT DOESN'T PAY WELL EITHER

ccording to recent U.S. statistics:
- Women now live 40 years longer than their grandmothers.
- The average time spent by American women in the paid work force used to be 20 years. That time has now increased to 36 years.
- More than 50 percent of all American women work now.
- An additional one million women enter the labor force each year.
- By 1990, it is estimated that close to 90 percent of all American men and women will be in the labor force.
- Ninety percent of working women are still concentrated in occupations which are low on the pay scale.
- Women make up the fastest growing poverty group in the nation.
- Eighty percent of America's poor are women and children. Many of these women are

displaced homemakers.
- Almost half of our nation's poor households are headed by women.
- Common-law marriages are considered illegal in most states.
- The divorce rate keeps climbing.
- Seventy-five percent of divorced women work.
- Alimony is becoming extinct.
- Child support, even when awarded to a divorced mother, is usually inadequate and is often impossible to collect.
- Women cannot afford to work overtime for extra pay because of the burden of their already heavy schedule of work at home.
- Thirty-three percent of the labor market is over age 45 now; most of the women have no pension of their own.

Consider these figures:
- Whereas men's earnings peak at ages 45-49, women's average earnings go downhill after ages 30-35.
- The average woman must work nine days to earn what the average man earns in five days.
- The average female college graduate's earnings are close to those of the average man with four years of high school - or less.

Add to these figures some other facts:
- There is discrimination in hiring: sex, age and marital status.
- Employers perceive any time out of the paid labor force as non-productive.
- Women still perform 90 percent of all housework and child care.

So, what does a woman want? Among other things, she wants the opportunity to earn money for the support of her family and for her own future security.

To do this, she needs:
- Training programs for decent, not dead-end, jobs.
- Flexible job hours.
- Adequate leaves, with job guarantees, to care for dependent family members.
- Round-the-clock child care centers to accomodate the needs of all working mothers.
- Family encouragement and cooperation.
- Equal pay for equal work.
- Equal pay for comparable job responsibilities.

This would be a good beginning!

The days are long gone when a woman worked for "pin money" or to while away the boring hours. We are serious about our work, about our <u>need</u> to work . . . and about our need to be <u>fairly</u> paid for it!

And what about the 45 million women in this country who do not receive any pay at all for their work?

What about the American homemaker?

39

HOMEMAKER:
A SERIOUS CHOICE

hat is a homemaker, anyway?

A homemaker is the person who uniquely establishes the tone and quality of the standard of living in one's home. S/he often is totally responsible for the complete care of the family's home, food, clothing, and health; and acts as secretary, business manager, counselor, and teacher.

I would love to have one. Wouldn't you?

How can the services of this paragon of helpfulness be obtained? There are only five ways:

1. Your parents may provide these things until you can do so yourself. Naturally, you are expected to contribute both your services and financial help as soon as you become capable of doing so.

2. Do it yourself. Move out and become your own homemaker.

3. Hire a person or persons to perform all

these services for you at the current market rate.

4. Enchant someone into serving you for nothing. (Lots of luck. Slavery never was very popular . . . particularly with the slaves.)

5. Enter a partnership agreement with your spouse: wherein s/he works as homemaker, while you provide the income. This is not a simple decision; it entails risk for both of you; and it is an expensive luxury.

Just as marrying, having children, and buying a home are joint decisions; so is the decision to have one of you shoulder the responsibilities as wage earner, while the other acts as homemaker. Of course, you may choose to share the responsibilities of wage earning and homemaking.

To discuss the subject and reach any logical conclusions, I will be bold enough to make one basic assumption, at this point: that you have had the good sense to marry your best friend. Therefore, you like each other. You enjoy each other's company. You laugh and have fun together. You respect each other. You feel a deep loyalty to each other. You love and care about your spouse as much as you care about yourself.

Please notice, I said, ". . . as much as you care about yourself." We are told, "Love your neighbor as you love yourself." No one ever said, "Love your neighbor instead of yourself."

Owing to the fact that statistics show that most men die 10-15 years sooner than women and many couples get divorced, most women will probably wind up alone in their later years. It does not sound like fun, but these are the facts.

Nevertheless, when you feel about your spouse the way I described, it is natural to want to spend the rest of your life together. Which makes it highly unlikely that you would deliberately arrange for one of you to kill yourself, working two or three jobs, while the other one takes it easy.

In other words, one way or another, you will want to distribute the work load evenly, so that the two of you can enjoy a long and happy life together.

How to decide? Who will be your homemaker?

Some decisions are made for us. If two paychecks are necessary to survive, for instance, both partners must be employed. The decision to share the burden of homemaking, in that case, seems a natural one. That way you would each be shouldering one and a half jobs.

It is when children enter the picture that choices become more difficult. Having, or being, a full-time homemaker is a luxury that many people simply cannot afford.

When children are small, what are your options for child care? Each parent taking turns, neighbors, grandparents, church, preschool? There is no easy way.

Suppose the children are in school while you are employed full-time. Does this mean you should expect yourself to handle three full-time jobs simultaneously: business woman all day, mother all evening, and housekeeper after that? Give yourself a break!

Whether you have a paying job or not, recognize the fact that you are valuable. Portion out the many demands on your time and energy with care.

Just as you respect other people's right to dignity and esteem, respect your own.

Choose who, and what, is important to YOU. Use your valuable time and energy to further YOUR goals. Of course, you have the right to give your time and work as a gift, if that is your choice. Do so only if you do it freely, willingly, and cheerfully. On the other hand, if you cannot bring yourself to give of your time and work enthusiastically, say "no." This requires no apology. Quite the contrary, your grudging continuation of an activity may prevent someone else's happy participation. In any case, a resentful gift has no merit.

For example, when my three oldest children were an infant and toddlers, a fund raiser asked me to cover six local blocks for contributions on a particular afternoon. A worthy cause. Terribly necessary. I was the only one who could help. Reluctant, I felt obliged not to refuse.

I was pregnant, as usual, and feeling none too spiffy. Not being able to afford a babysitter, I bundled everyone up, took the stroller, and struggled down our two flights of stairs. Of course, it began to drizzle when we were at the most distant point from home, so I decided I might as well finish; we continued plodding from house to house.

Grumbling and exhausted, I dragged all the crying children upstairs in time to answer our ringing phone. A neighbor, whom I did not know, called to say how disappointed she was that I had taken away her job. She looked forward to collecting for this charity each year. It was her one chance to get out and meet the neighbors . . . and I had spoiled it.

So much for using my head and respecting my own honest feelings.

It requires humility to admit that we have limitations. If you are not as strong as an Amazon, do not undertake severely strenuous tasks. If you are physically vulnerable, have the good sense not to destroy the equipment you have left.

Get acquainted with your body and its needs. If it requires six or seven or nine hours rest each night to operate efficiently, provide it. If it needs regular exercise to maintain sufficient energy, put that on your priority list. This is one of those tasks that you cannot delegate.

Value your energy. If ardently complaining pessimists consistently drain the batteries of your optimism, avoid those people. Since your continued listening to their complaints does nothing to alleviate or change their dismal point of view, be aware of the fact that you cannot afford to let your energies be drained so low, lest you endanger your own spirit.

You owe allegiance to your own goals. Suppose a clean house (or anything else) were rated on a scale of one to ten (with "ten" suitable for Better Homes and Gardens, and "one" merely livable.) Clean the house to the number that suits your goals, because YOU choose to do so, not because your mother, your husband, society, or "they" insist you must. It is not "their" business.

If you have children, it is your job to guide them to adulthood. This duty does not permit allowing them to behave as little children until age twenty-one. It entails putting into their hands such responsibilities as they can effectively manage, little by little.

Of course, it is more work for you, initially, than it would be just to do the job, yourself. But there is no other way they can learn. If your goals include having your children mature into capable, loving, responsible adults, it is your job to have them learn and practice this as they grow. This means insisting that they have the same respect for your time and work as they have for others'.

In summary, we have defined the identity, and some of the responsibilities and goals, of the homemaker. The most significant question regarding homemakers is: who decides that you should be one? In the case of a married couple, it would be a joint decision that one party would contribute his/her share of the partnership work in the home environment. By that same decision, the other person would work elsewhere for money. Both partners would share equally the benefits of their own and each other's labor: a comfortable home, money, children, etc.

I emphasize this to dispel the <u>widespread, erroneous belief</u> that only work which earns dollars has value.

While it's true that a person earns no money performing her own tasks as wife-mother-homemaker, this is NOT to be construed as an indication of her worth - or lack of worth.

On the contrary, the homemaker's work is <u>so</u> valuable that if one had to hire outside help to do each task performed in the home at current pay rates. . . who could afford it?

Most people expect a fair day's pay for a fair day's work. It is then each person's responsibility to save for his retirement. Where does that leave the average homemaker? The fact is that if the homemaker is to have any kind of secure future, lack of money in her own name is a serious situation which she must change!

40

SHOULD A HOMEMAKER SEEK A CAREER?

e often feel that the choice between being a homemaker or a member of the paid work force is forced upon us by circumstance.

On the other hand, some of us just seem to drift into one lifestyle or another. There is a better way to choose a profession; examine your circumstances carefully, decide what you really WANT to do, and make a deliberate choice. Then make the most of what you have.

We all have the opportunity to make our lives better than they are now. We can effect change if we want to. We, ourselves, can act on our own behalf; in doing so, we can improve the lives of others, as well as our own.

I address the 55 percent of American women who are now in paid employment as well as the 45 percent of this country's working women who are NOT being paid: the homemakers.

What is wrong with being a homemaker? The job is undervalued by society at large because it

does not provide the material benefits that are found in a good bona fide job:
- Interesting, challenging work
- Full appreciation for work well done (money, fame, respect, applause)
- A feeling of participation in decision making
- Opportunity for advancement
- Job security
- Insurance (health, disability, life)
- Retirement pension in your own name

All this is absolutely true. Does that mean, "Down with homemaking and mothering?" Of course not. That would be like throwing the baby out with the bath water.

What is right with being a wife-mother-homemaker? Performing the job with excellence is still one of the most important, meaningful tasks a woman can accomplish . . . for herself, her family, her community and the world. What I propose is a way to do that while managing to incorporate some of the advantages of any other decent job. Benefits that, up to now, have been denied women who have chosen the domestic life, can be earned . . . if we handle our skills in a businesslike manner.

Women are urged, "Get a CAREER", by feminists, sociologists, psychologists, and economists. It sounds sensible on paper.

However, even though they are intelligent, sensible and competent, many homemakers find it impractical to pursue a job outside their home, much less a career.

Faced with this circumstance, how can today's homemaker hope to gain any degree of physical, financial, intellectual, psychological or spiritual independence?

Initially, when the homemaker considers joining the wage earners, she should ask herself these questions.

1. What is there that I can do as well as, or better than, anybody else to earn money?
2. Is there a realistic market for it? Can I create one?
3. What would I need for this job in terms of education, transportation, wardrobe, equipment, supplies, dues, and meals?
4. What would these things cost?
5. What income would be possible?
6. After deducting income tax, social security tax, child care expense, extra household expenses incurred due to my absence, what would be left?
7. How many extra hours of labor is it going to cost me to net this amount?
8. Is it worth it to me in terms of the tax on my energy, my state of mind, and my personal satisfaction?
9. How much can I count on the cooperation of my family?
10. Does the job provide the opportunity to grow and advance?
11. Does it provide necessary health, disability and life insurance?

Obviously, it would be nonproductive to knock yourself out for negative rewards. Therefore, count up all the costs and all the rewards before making any final decision. After all, you want to improve your position, not make it worse.

After investigating all the possibilities and their ramifications, you may conclude that you cannot afford to work outside your home. You may discover that you would not be able to command a salary large enough to yield sufficient money to cover all the expenses that having the job would incur.

If that is the case, you had better knuckle down to being the best money manager the world has ever seen.

1. Learn to budget whatever income you may have.
2. SAVE! Pay yourself first. Aim to save ten percent right off the top before anything else.
3. Comparison shop and unit price for everything.
4. Do not spend what you cannot afford.
5. If you use a credit card, pay the bill in full before accruing any finance charges.
6. Look ahead, set savings goals for auto, house, college, vacation, retirement fund, etc.
7. Keep developing your abilities, not only for your self-satisfaction, but also to improve your position.

41

CARE GIVER:
PRAISE INSTEAD OF PAY

are givers are essential to civilization.

Some examples of care givers are nurses, teachers, rearers of children and homemakers. These positions are mostly staffed by women who receive high praise for their worthy labor. Society, however, seems to think that praise is an adequate substitute for financial reward. It is not.

Nurses are paid far less than their worth. They may soon unite, unionize, negotiate, and/or strike for more realistic compensation for their challenging, difficult, life-saving work.

Caretakers of other people's children also suffer, at present, from unrealistic, unjustly low recompense for their important jobs.

WARNING!

SOME OF THE FOLLOWING SITUATIONS
MAY ENDANGER YOUR LIFE!

The homemaker is at the very bottom of the job-reward scale. She can work 20 hours a day, caring for her own husband, children, and home . . . and earn no money at all. Her work has intrinsic value. It is not only necessary, but immediately vital to the well-being of her family, to the community and to the world.

However, she is a person, like anyone else, who must look to her own needs, as well as the needs of others. Some day she will be "unemployed" when her husband is gone, and her children are out on their own. By then she may have been out of the paid work force for 10-30 years. She will be middle-aged with no income, no pension and, perhaps, no insurance. That is serious trouble. And her future looks even dimmer.

She could continue to perform her valuable job as homemaker-wife-mother with more peace of mind if she got paid for work, like everyone else. But where would the money come from?

From her husband? That puts her in the position of complete dependence with her fate in the benevolent, capable, generous, faithful, healthy, living hands of another. If he is, and continues to be, all of these good things, she may be fine.

There is no guarantee that he will remain any of these things. In which case, she again faces a desperate future. Eighty percent of our nation's poor are women and children.

It has been suggested that the government pay mother-homemakers. I hate to be a wet blanket regarding this pipe dream, but be realistic. You and I know that one cannot spend what one does not have. The government does not seem to know it; we do. Our federal government has enough trouble with the national debt without paying homemakers.

There is only one way a woman at home is going to acquire the money necessary for her own future security. She must take the responsibility, herself. She cannot afford not to.

Consider the following reasoning:

As a mature, intelligent woman, I do what I must for my family and me to survive in as healthy and happy a manner as possible. That may include paid work, or it may not. Whichever course I follow, it is the one I deem best at the time for me. It is my life . . . I am responsible for my own decisions.

Regardless of ideologies, some truths are unchanging:
- If I wish to have a family, I must have a mate.
- Unless we inherit a fortune, one or both of us must earn a wage.
- If we are to have children, I, the woman, must bear them.
- If children exist, someone must care for them until they can care for themselves.

No one lives forever; statistically, I will outlast my mate by 10-15 years, divorce notwithstanding.

Also, statistically, 80 percent of our nation's poor are women and children.

Therefore, looking ahead, if I wish to avoid becoming a burden to my children, I must assume the responsibility of providing for my own care in my later years.

This will require, among other things, health insurance, living expenses and as much savings as I can manage to accumulate.

Thus, whatever my future goals may include, from this moment on, I have as my concurrent goal the saving and the investing of money for my own future. It is my responsibility to myself and to my family.

If I have the option to choose to remain out of the paid work force for 5-15-25 or more years, I must realize that this choice entails risk.

The risk involves the possibility that one option may no longer be available to me. My job opportunities are likely to decrease as my age and years of unemployment increase.

Thus, although most women seek employment because they need the money instantly, or for personal satisfaction, retaining their employability for future options may be another very good reason for them to remain employed, at least part-time, if not full-time.

Although I may not need employment now, I must look ahead and realize that its' prolonged postponement puts me in serious danger. This danger remains present unless, and until, I can manage to save sufficient retirement funds, from my mate's wages, during the time that I work in our home without pay.

Furthermore, if my mate retains, within his person, the VALUABLE COMMODITY of all of his earning power, I strongly recommend having OUR own retirement funds (not to be confused with his company's pension plan) in my name (with spouse as beneficiary). This is because, according to our joint decision, I am relinquishing my own earning power by choosing to channel my life's work in an unpaid capacity: creating and sustaining a high-quality, happy, healthy home.

At least, I should have equal retirement assets in my own name. Consider I.R.A., Keogh, or just plain savings from ordinary family income, invested to earn growth and interest.

In any case, my secure future will have to be planned and taken care of by me . . . or I may not have one.

ATTENTION!

IF YOU ARE NOT SUFFICIENTLY ALARMED BY THE PRECEEDING INFORMATION . . . . . .

READ IT AGAIN!

42

HOW TO SUCCEED IN BUSINESS AT HOME IN THE WORK OF YOUR CHOICE

an it be done? Yes, it can.

How To Succeed

Success, by definition, is getting what you want: happiness, fame, fortune, or anything else. However, you stand little chance of getting what you want if you do not know what you are looking for.

So, first, identify your goal . . . or goals. Ask yourself these questions; then write down your honest answers.

1. Who am I? Consider your many and varied roles: person, daughter, sister, friend, wife, mother, artist, church member, homemaker, quilter, business professional, athlete, etc.

2. What do I already have? Count your

blessings and your accomplishments.
3. What do I want? Physically, psychologically, intellectually, spiritually, financially, etc.
4. What is their order of importance?
5. Which are long term and which are short term goals?
6. What is keeping me from having these things now? Consider lack of time, education, money, research, physical fitness, family cooperation and/or understanding, etc.
7. What steps can I take to overcome these obstacles in order to attain my goals? List in chronological order.
8. What is a realistic time limit for achieving each of these steps.

Re-evaluate these every 6-12 months.

Now that you know what you want, and before jumping willy-nilly into a business, ask yourself: "Will it get me what I want? Am I any good at it? Is there a market for it?" Research the market, the competition, your location, the economy, all the possibilities.

If I enjoy quilting, for instance, and decide to do it professionally, I should compare the projected results with my goals.

If what I seek is happiness, will my enjoyment be ruined by being pressed for time and feeling pushed to produce what other people want, instead of what I, the artist, personally find beautiful?

If my goal is money, will my earning capabilities match my needs? If I have no other source of income, I cannot afford to use my time, energy and effort working for minimum wages.

If I want to be publicly recognized for my accomplishments, will I be able to achieve this by my quilting?

The Work of Your Choice

If you are responsible for your family's primary source of income, you have little, or no, time to experiment. You need a decent income right now, in addition to adequate life, disability and health insurance. That usually means you must aggressively pursue whatever kind of job that can yield the greatest income immediately.

If you do not particularly enjoy the kind of work you find at first, try to prepare yourself for the type of job you would like. Go to night school, study on your own, or do whatever is necessary to accomplish this goal. But do not just continue in the unsatisfactory job, grumbling and doing nothing to improve yourself. That will only bring you ulcers, headaches, little or no sympathy, and certainly not your ideal position.

Frequently, the choice to earn money at home is made by women who need to be there for young children or ailing family.

If you have been out of the paid work force for some time, re-entry could be hindered due to:
- rusty or outdated skills,
- chronic physical ailments (aching joints, etc.),
- the erroneous perception of many employers that unpaid work has no value.

In any case, working at home, part-time, at your own convenience, being close at hand to family, may be an ideal choice if you already have adequate insurance and another primary source of income.

Quilting, as a hobby turned business, might, indeed, prove to be a means of earning a supplementary income and providing pleasure and, possibly, fame.

Hobby Versus Business

When your hobby income exceeds your hobby expenses, your net earnings are taxable; provided you meet the requirements of filing a form 1040 tax return. And, if that hobby activity nets $400 or more per year, you are also required to pay social security (F.I.C.A.) tax.

It is only when you conduct your hobby as a business and fill out a Schedule C for the I.R.S. that you are permitted to deduct all quilting supplies and expenses, advertising, pertinent study, books, travel and fees from your gross quilting income. This leaves only the smaller net figure upon which you must pay tax.

You will be surprised to discover, once you start keeping track of all your expenditures, just how quickly they do mount. With a hobby, you could easily spend hundreds of dollars a year on quilting related items, using money from the family budget. Whereas, with a business, you may cover all those expenses by earning that amount from your quilting efforts, knowing that your otherwise-very-expensive hobby is paying for itself.

Furthermore, if you can net up to $2,000 annually, over and above your expenses and you can afford to do without spending it, put that money into an Individual Retirement Account (I.R.A.) and you can defer paying taxes on it until age 59-1/2 to 70, depending upon when you decide to begin drawing it out. Check current law for possible change.

If you are a homemaker without earned income, you are permitted to put $250 into an I.R.A. annually with your spouse. In order to raise that I.R.A. contribution to $2,000, the stipulation is that you must earn it.

Now $2,000 may not seem like a great deal of money. But did you know that an investment of $2,000 annually at a yield of 10 percent a year, started when you were 30, would build to $400,000 by the time you are 59-1/2? And, unlike life insurance, it will be yours to enjoy at that time even without someone having to die.

All these reasons combine to provide you with a high incentive, not only to earn, but to report and invest those earnings.

It should be noted that your quilting must show a profit for two out of five years in order to be considered a business. Hobby losses are not deductible. (Again, check current law.)

Helpful Hints
for the Wife-Mother-Homemaker

1. Earn public recognition for your efforts to achieve credibility with your family (who otherwise might think, "Why are you fooling around with your little hobby, instead of doing something important, like fixing supper, laundering clothes, darning socks, baking desserts?") Seek recognition and appreciation, such as good grades, awards, publicity, and money.

2. Only do housekeeping chores when family is witness, lest they continue in their popular, but erroneous, belief that such deeds are performed by elves and good fairies during the night while the family sleeps.

3. Only accept responsibility for those tasks that you can perform with enthusiasm, or **refuse**. Just because three committees ask you to make cookies for bake sales, at a time when you are facing quilting deadlines, does not mean you have to do it. Give yourself permission to say, "No".

4. Share goals with your family. Talk to your husband. Tell him how you feel. Share with him your enthusiasm for your goals. After all, he is probably part of them. Write your goals on paper like an outline or a map, listing the steps that lead toward them. Post it on the family bulletin board for all to see. As you accomplish each step, cross it off so that your family can see what you are working for. Put your daily "To Do" list on the kitchen table and cross off each chore. The family needs to see that you have not been "wasting your time", but are working toward those definite goals.

5. Share the homemaking load. Everyone lives in your home, everyone can proudly take part in the care of it. Ask for volunteers;

delegate or assign necessary housekeeping chores so that you, too, may have time to pursue your goals.

Once you delegate tasks to people, let them do them. Be firm about this. Lower your standards at first, if necessary. Show your appreciation for their efforts just as you would like the family to acknowledge and appreciate your efforts when you do the tasks. Organize chores and let the family have a say, too.

6. Respect your energy; acknowledge your limitations. Plan strenuous jobs during your peak energy times. Do not bite off more than you can comfortably chew. For instance, do you really want to promise that you will create one quilt per week?

7. Respect your work. You are the expert. There will be times when good judgment will require refusing certain jobs. I have acquired a satisfaction-guaranteed attitude over the years. I remind myself of the sign in the elegant glassware department: "You ruin it: you buy it." It encourages me to do very careful work.

There is no substitute for good communication. I write down what my customers ask for and show them the placement, color, size and shape of the design. I estimate the price and get a deposit. I promise a date of completion and I deliver exactly what I promised, at, or before, the appointed time. If they are not satisfied after all that, then it is their problem.

8. Respect your time. Keep track of all chargeable time required for each quilt, or other job. Record all expenses. Investigate competition. Set prices commensurate with your skill that will add to the desirability of your product.

You do not want to be unrealistically high, and price yourself out of business. Neither do you want to work for nothing.

9. Respect yourself. If you do not, why should anyone else?

In summary, can you expect to succeed in business at home in the work of your choice? The answer is certainly, "Yes", provided your expectations are realistic.

- -

Review The Following

Ask yourself:

- Who am I? What are my many roles?
- What do I already have?
- What do I want? (Physically, psychologically, intellectually, spiritually, financially, etc.)
- What is their order of importance?
- Which are long term? Short term?
- What is standing in my way now?
- What can I do to overcome these obstacles? List steps in chronological order.
- What is a realistic time limit for achievement of each step?

Re-evaluate this list every 6-12 months.

Additional check list for success:

- Will this goal (job) make me happy?
- Am I any good at it?
- Is there a market for it?
- Will the work, itself, give me pleasure?
- Will it yield enough money to make it worthwhile?
- Will it make me famous, or at least known, for my good work?

Choosing your work:

If you are your family's primary source of income, you have no choice. You cannot even consider part-time work. You must seek the highest paying job you can find which provides health, disability and life insurance.

If you don't like the job, try to get a better one. Become more highly qualified.

If you can only work part-time and find it difficult to work outside your home, a home-based business might work for you.

Hobby turned business:

When it comes to reporting income on your tax return, every detail counts. Read text carefully for this.

Helpful Hints for the wife-mother-entrepreneur:

- Earn public recognition such as good grades, awards and/or money to achieve credibility with your family.

- <u>Only do housekeeping chores when family is witness.</u>
  Think about this one.
- Respect your goals. Give YOUR goals as much, or more, priority as you give those of other people.
  Give yourself permission to say, "No".
- Share your goals with your family. Make goals visible.
- Share the homemaking load. Show appreciation for a job well done; but once a person is assigned a job, LET HIM DO IT.
- Respect your energy and acknowledge your limitations.
- Respect your work.
- Respect your time.
- Respect yourself!

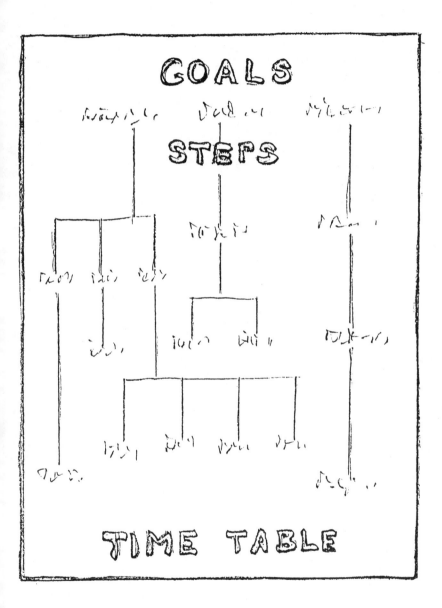

PART V

Getting It Together

43

SELF ESTEEM FOR A VALUABLE AND IRREPLACEABLE PERSON: YOU

nce there was a fair maiden who waited all her life for a shining armored knight on a white horse.

She wound up cleaning up after the horse.

Then there was the ostrich, who buried her head in the sand, thinking, "If I hide, nothing can hurt me."

Finally, there was a generous, thoughtful, kind, loving woman, who thought of herself as last in line for consideration for so long, that everyone else thought that way, too. She became sad when people treated her like the doormat that she imitated.

The moral of these stories is: one's life is far too precious to waste, to hide, or to allow it to be trampled upon.

It is a matter of self-esteem.

While it is true that our feelings are reflected in our actions, so also can our actions influence our thoughts and feelings. If we take the initiative and act as if we have self-esteem, we begin to think and feel that way, too.

For a woman to hold herself in low esteem is a great mistake. Not only is such an attitude nonproductive; it is poor judgment. Each of us is a total person made up of spirit, mind and body . . . valuable and irreplaceable.

Our spirit, which we share with God and each other, is our true Self, and resides within our subconscious. We can tap into our spirit regularly with our conscious mind for creative ideas, for comfort and for assurance on those occasions when our conscious minds reach their temporarily limited capacity.

Our minds, on the other hand, control our sense of identity, our conscious thinking, our attitude, our knowledge, and our appreciation of our Selves.

"Well, if our minds are so perfect," you might ask, "why do we stumble around most of the time, working at half steam?" Chances are, you just answered your own question. Most of us are using only a fraction of our capabilities.

The important thing is, don't compare yourself with anyone else. Just be the best YOU that you can be.

Love yourself for the good and valuable person that you are!

44

GOD LOVES ME

irtues run wild can sometimes be destructive.

Take the virtue of humility, for instance. If a person is an overbearing, pompous, egotistical, self-righteous, conceited bore, that person could certainly do with a good stiff dose of humility.

Most women are not lacking in this virtue; they are **drowning** in it.

Many displaced homemakers need training just to apply for a job. Mothers need to be role models for daughters who must prepare to be financially independent. And working women still need assertiveness training to ask for a simple raise.

For goodness' sake, what these women **need** is a boost in self-confidence, NOT another lecture on humility.

Yet, once again I heard the same old sermon from the pulpit last week, exhorting us to be more humble. I wanted to groan, "Give me a break! How about some words of encouragement, some inspiration to get through the next week?"

I mentioned it to my husband and to my young adult daughter who is assertive to the point of having a first degree brown belt in Karate. "Oh, you're just finding fault, Mom," she protested.

I wonder if men and younger women can even understand what I'm talking about.

As a woman over thirty, I have been taught:
- O Lord, I am not worthy.
- The meek shall inherit the earth.
- God first, everyone else second, me last.
- All good things come to her who waits.
- Have faith; God will provide.

These are all good ideas, aren't they?

Now, try imagining these same ideas as your basic training for a sales position. You'd be a dead duck, wouldn't you!?

When a woman enters and tries to succeed in the work force, she is definitely in a sales position. She's either selling herself as a capable employee, marketing her skills, or selling her company's product or services.

It follows, as the night follows the day, that she will never succeed with that "I-am-not-worthy" attitude.

In fact, too much of that attitude is not even mentally healthy. Psychologists tell us that one of the main symptoms of depression is an overwhelming feeling of unworthiness, a lack of self-esteem.

If we are too humble, we cannot function as normal, mentally healthy people.

Each of us needs self-esteem, a feeling of self-worth. We have to LOVE OURSELVES and

LIKE OURSELVES in order to share these same good feelings with others.

So please, unless you feel you really need more, the next time some good soul preaches to you about humility, don't pay too much mind. Just turn the other cheek and say to yourself, "I am made in God's own image. God loves me and I am wonderful!"

45

WHO IS YOUR SELF?

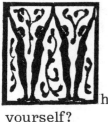ho do you talk to when you talk to yourself?

Doctors know that we use our larynx and throat muscles, even when we are not speaking aloud. The reason is that, because we normally communicate with language, we have developed the habit of following a conscious line of thought with words, even though we are silent.

When we say, "I had a talk with myself", we know that the speaker, the talker, is our conscious mind.

But who do you talk to? God? Your guardian angel? Or is it your spirit-soul-SELF? The inner SELF, which is your true aliveness. The invisible true SELF, which makes you, YOU.

When you die, your body remains behind. Friends and family gather for a last farewell. You are the reason for the gathering, but they visit with each other, not you. Why? Because your meaningful essence, your true spirit-soul, YOU are no longer apparent. The important part of you, your SELF, sheds the body, and goes on (we assume) to bigger and better things.

Right now, however, your body and spirit SELF are working together, so that when you say, "I really have to have a talk with my SELF," you truly mean, "My conscious mind really has to get together with my inner SELF."

We often get so caught up with the details of day to day living, we neglect our spirit SELVES. Then what happens? Our conscious minds, all bogged down with routine trivia, start pulling in different directions than our inner SELVES wish to go. We feel torn apart and frayed at the edges; we begin to unravel.

That is when we have to call a halt and say, "Now, hear this. This pulling in different directions is getting us nowhere. At this rate, none of us is going to survive. Starting now, the three of us (mind, body, and inner SELF) have to get it together. This is what we are going to do." Then you can proceed to issue proper, positive directions for the manner in which you wish your SELF to proceed.

Of course, if you are not used to having these conversations with your SELF, if you have spent your whole life, up to now, just drifting along with the current, this whole idea of taking control of your life (for that is what it is) might seem a little strange.

Think of it. Would it not be nice, for a change, for you to be in the driver's seat with you making the plans and giving directions instead of just waiting at everyone else's beck and call? Have you always been **told** what to do and when to do it? Have you ever thought of being in charge of your life?

Does it sound scary? Have you always had a boss to tell you how to live your life? What would happen if the boss was not there some day? Would you be able to make your own decisions?

Taking charge might seem strange, at first, to people who have never really thought much about directing their own lives. But, once you have tried it, you will never go back to being a puppet.

How does one go about taking charge?

All you need is to have confidence in your SELF!

46

USE YOUR HEAD, THE WHOLE THING

ach half of the brain controls muscle coordination for the opposite side of the body.

This much we knew many years ago. What are the other aspects of right-left brain activity? Is there really anything to it? How does it relate to us personally?

A brain is important; everyone has one. When it ceases to function, you are dead. Doctors have seen dead or damaged brains; scientists have studied abnormal ones. Yet oddly enough, only in the last decade or so has anyone tried to do comprehensive studies on the function of normal brains.

The statement that we only use 10 to 20 percent of our brains has always suggested to me the questions, "Who says so? Where is it written? Where does it say that the brain has exactly such and such measurable capacity?"

Scientists are puzzled by the same questions. In all their research they have been amazed that they have not yet discovered the capacity of a normal brain. Not of a genius, mind you, but just a normal brain. It seems that, so far, studies have only shown limitless capacities for normal brains.

So why are we not all geniuses? Good question. Apparently <u>the brain, like muscle,</u> gets rusty with nonuse, but <u>thrives with constant exercise</u>. A person of any age, with little, or no, mental stimulation will soon exhibit all the liveliness and excitement of a turnip. Yet, give that person new challenges to stimulate curiosity with proper rewards to encourage it and a <u>normal, healthy person can enjoy mental growth all her life long</u>.

Fairly recently, 20-30 years is "fairly recent", it was discovered that, though they are connected, the two halves of the brain, right and left, are capable of working independently. Each has the capacity to know, to make decisions, and to initiate action while operating in distinctly different modes.

The left half relates information in linear patterns, like an outline or a computer. It organizes with words and plans a logical course of action; but, it cannot generate new ideas. The right half knows things instinctively, feels strong hunches, and becomes aware of an idea suddenly; but, it cannot express with words how it was done.

Keeping in mind that the brain's efficiency increases the more it is used, we can more easily understand the reasons for some behavioral patterns. When a person's education and occupation have constantly stressed left brain activity (math, and other exact sciences) to the exclusion of all else, it is not surprising to find a lack of creativity, imagination and visualization. On the other hand, when a person has had to depend on her right brain capacities for years, (caring for small children, for instance) it is possible that the left half will have suffered from lack of exercise.

"Creative accounting" sounds just about as sensible as a "logical infant." Did you ever try to reason with a four year old? That is about as productive as reassuring an I.R.S. agent that you arrived at a certain figure on a hunch.

In other words, each half of our brain provides a good and useful method of accomplishing some things. To utilize only one-half of our brain exclusively is to cut our total capacity in half.

There was a time when we were expected to repeat the lives of our parents. Remember? He was born a winemaker, just like his father, and his father's father before him. There was also a time when a person could return home after ten or twenty years absence, and find few changes. Not any more. It used to be said that death and taxes were the only things you could count on. Well, we had better add one more thing: death, taxes, and change. Certainly, our generation has seen the growing necessity of being adaptable; and the generation of our children will know no other way of life.

Thus, in the time of our own parents, it might have been acceptable and sufficient to operate at "half steam", as it were, using only one main pattern of thinking. However, recent events have made it clear that we need to use all our capabilities in order to succeed. I am not just speaking of excelling; I am talking about surviving.

Business owners who never have any new ideas, or who ignore people's feelings, will soon go out of business. By the same token, a woman cannot use the excuse, "I just have no head for business," and expect to be taken care of any more.

The period of a few decades ago has been nostalgically referred to as a "simpler time." Perhaps. Increasingly rapid improvements in communication and transportation have caused the world, in a sense, to become smaller. Events occurring in one place are no longer isolated, but can instantaneously affect people the world over. The probability of our world changing even more rapidly, from this point on, will demand our utmost abilities to adapt swiftly and well if we are to survive to live a rich and meaningful life.

Those of us in the business world must incorporate creative new approaches to problem solving, both on the production line and in attitudes toward employees. Appreciation, respect and sensitivity are every bit as important to company success as quotas and "bottom lines."

People not in the paid work force will face challenges, too. A woman who has spent years successfully rearing a family is in for many drastic changes that will require all her resources, including whole brain activity, in order to have a productive, challenging life.

Actually, if a mother has done her job well in preparing her children to be independent, she will literally work her way out of a job. As a wife and homemaker, she may spend all of her time and energy in a supportive role to her husband's career. Even though such a situation forces financial dependence upon her, it may be expedient, and temporarily mutually beneficial, if his career provides the best economic support for the family.

However, because both these consuming occupations of wife and mother can come to an end at a time when she has the whole second half of her life to live, she is faced with tremendous changes. Many of these can be overwhelming, unless she bravely prepares herself to take charge of her future.

Think of it! This is great news!

Every scientific community which has studied the average brain has agreed on one thing: the average person has unlimited capacities.

You already have this great potential within you.

<u>Reach for it!</u>

Tap into it!

USE IT!

47

FEELING FIT AND LOOKING FINE

FEELING FIT

hysical fitness implies a great deal more than just not being sick.

It's the joy of stretching strong muscles, moving limber joints, and of breathing deeply with healthy lungs. Physical fitness is having the energy to rise each day with the enthusiasm to tackle new challenges.

Illness or injury can befall any one of us at any time. This moves us to action to cure those same ills and injuries. But don't wait until something goes wrong before you take action. Put physical exercise at the top of your daily priority list, or at least on three days a week.

The kind of exercise I suggest is 30-40 minutes of any sort of physical activity which gets your heart pumping, your blood moving and your lungs working. Choose an activity that's fun; one that you enjoy. Add to this 5-30 minutes of daily stretching exercises. Do them smoothly, evenly, gently with no bouncing to loosen and limber up stiff joints. (Check with your doctor before beginning your exercise program.)

You say you "don't have time?"

Do you give so much attention to the needs of your family that you neglect your own needs?

Keep in mind that just as you work to develop your mind, spirit and self-esteem, you must do the same to keep your body in good condition.

Feeling fit and looking fine do wonders for your morale and self-confidence.

LOOKING FINE

The way to look your best on the outside is to be aware of exactly who you are on the inside: a terrific and beautiful person! Then create your image accordingly.

This, however, requires a plan. And if the first plan doesn't work, get another one.

Plan A for "looking fine" is to have God create you absolutely gorgeous.

Failing that, Plan B is to take long-term measures. Exercise, shed twenty pounds, have your teeth straightened, or schedule that repair surgery you've been postponing. These are all good steps that will take time.

Meanwhile, you can put Plan C to work. It requires that you take inventory of all your physical assets and liabilities. Then take action to accentuate the positives and camouflage the negatives.

Following are some Do's and Don'ts on how to do exactly that.

Hair: Treat yourself to a good cut, shaped to compliment your face, neck and profile. Style it for easy care. Keep it clean and well brushed to make it shine. (Cover grey, if you like.)

Figure: Choose design lines and textures to flatter your figure.

Face: Keep your skin clean and pores tight. Use cleanser, moisturizer and astringent as necessary. Use make-up sparingly to enhance your own natural coloring. Wear foundation only if you must, to smooth out unevenness of color (not to cover blemishes).

Do use lip color and blusher; two of the nicest things you can do for yourself.

Use concealer (underneath the eyes) if necessary, brow pencil, shadow and perhaps mascara.

Wardrobe: What is the perfect wardrobe? One that will provide the maximum number of coordinated looks with the least number of pieces. The ideal wardrobe should enable you to pack enough clothing into a medium sized suitcase for a week-long stay in San Francisco (hot during the day and cold at night); clothing that you can take off or layer on, in which you will look appropriate at all times.

Choose **styles** to suit your personality and your activities.

Color can serve two purposes. It can coordinate your clothing for a year or more. And it can flatter you by making your complexion appear healthy and glowing and your hair bright and shining (or dark and rich).

Weed out all excess items and add only those pieces necessary to achieve your perfect wardrobe.

Plan C is ideal for the person who wants to make the most of her best RIGHT NOW!

NATURAL DAYTIME MAKE-UP

Selection: Do this on a bright, sunny day in the full light of a north window using at least a foot-square mirror.

Foundation: Choose a color that is closest in hue and value to the overall appearance of your whole face. (If you have many dark freckles, choose a color closer to the background color of your face . . . not the color of your freckles.)

Concealer: By all means, conceal dark circles beneath the eyes. Again, use the same overall color of your face.

Blusher: Pinch one cheek. Select blusher which makes the other cheek match.

Lip color: A little deeper and brighter than your lips. Coordinate hue with blusher and clothing.

Eye shadow: Matte finish. Fair complexions: Choose either your darkest or medium hair color to blend with lashes and brows or choose a plum-taupe tone which will enhance the hue of your eyelids. Apply color on upper lid, close to lashes. Then gently smudge the edges, blending the shadow to the outer, upper edges of your lids. This will make your eyes appear larger and brighter. For darker complexions: You'll need to experiment with color. The idea is to achieve the illusion of beauty with a natural and flattering look.

Take care. An obviously artificial look is a distraction, not a compliment.

Additional hint: I suggest two separate sets of blusher, lip color and eye shadow; one of warm coordinated colors and one of cooler shades . . . to be worn with clothing of either warm or cool hues.

GLOW WITH COLOR

You can, you know.

You can either glow brightly and beautifully or fade and disappear completely, depending on the colors surrounding you.

The funny thing, or maybe not so funny, is that most of us have no idea how we appear to others.

We look in the mirror for certain information:
- Does my hair look OK?
- Hemline straight?
- Do I need make-up?

Few of us realize the marvelous difference color has on our appearance.

"What's so important about our appearance?" you might ask, since I've been telling you that it's a person's attitude that's most important. The key is that all parts of our whole selves are interrelated. If we can make ourselves look great and are truly conscious of our terrific appearance, we soon feel that way, too.

If you wake up on a drizzly, cold, greyish morning with limp, greyish hair, and a limp, greyish face and put on limp, greyish clothes, what are you going to see when you pass by the inevitable mirror? A limp, grey person with a limp, grey attitude to match the cold, grey, drizzly day!

Now, envision this, instead. Same morning, same person.

271

You arrange your hair as attractively as possible.

You select well-fitting clothing appropriate for your day's activities, in colors that make your face appear to glow with health and make your hair appear bright and shining.

You apply just enough make-up, not to change your coloring, but to enhance your own natural good looks.

Now, whenever you happen to pass a mirror, you'll say to yourself, "All **right**! Looking GOOD!"

Believe me, THAT does wonderful things for your attitude, how you feel about yourself and your overall self-confidence.

Knowing you look good can be a great morale booster. But just how does color affect our appearance? How does it work?

Did you ever stop to think what a large part color plays in giving clues to the state of our health? Think about the "colorful" and accurately descriptive comments, especially regarding the face:

"White as a ghost"
"Blue with cold"
"Red with embarrassment"
"Grey as death"
"Purple with rage"

Notice that none of these expressions stipulate what color (hue) a person's face actually happens to be? They are statements about the general effect of a person's appearance! In other words, a snap judgment of one's perception of another's well-being.

Color is not, in itself, a substance. It is more like a phenomenon, or a happening, which requires the coordination of mind, eye and light. Our minds perceive . . . what our eyes see . . . with the aid of light.

Let's talk briefly about each of these three things: eyes, light and perception.

Since we are all "on the inside, looking out," our own eyes are the only equipment we have. A small number of us are color-blind to some degree. Nothing will change that. What each person perceives is reality for that person.

Light sources differ vastly in color (hue) as well as brightness. To accomplish any important color comparisons, I recommend noon daylight in light shade . . . or the closest thing to it.

That leaves perception as the last variable. We do not view objects in total isolation; in a vacuum, as it were. We see them in their setting. That is, we see a person's wrapping (clothing) at the same instant we observe her face. And, we are immediately aware of the comparison between the two.

Her face appears darker or lighter (value), duller or brighter (intensity), and more or less "yellow" or "red" (or whatever - that is, hue) than her clothing. This is an observable optical illusion known as "simultaneous contrast."

Obviously, a person's face doesn't change color, chameleon-like, as she changes her blouse - but our perception of it does!

THE COLOR CONSULTATION

When I have a color consultation with a client, I attempt to give her a crash course on color and all its observable effects on her appearance. I do it in such a way that afterward, she will be able to identify, not just the 250-300 colors that we have used, but, any color. She will be able to decide not only, "Is it flattering?" but also "Why?" or "Why not?" as well.

I divide the session into several parts. We begin with the client's face bare of make-up.

Personal Coloring: With 80 or more colored fabrics, I drape her shoulders to find and cut small samples that match her <u>complexion</u>, her <u>hair</u> and her <u>eyes</u>; usually there are three to five colors in each group. (By the way, I have male clients, too.)

Make-up: Looking at the fabric color samples, I point out hues of blusher, lip color, eye shadow (and perhaps hair color) that do not CHANGE her own natural coloring, but merely ENHANCE it.

Then I ask her to apply the make-up. If her complexion is less than even, she can use a base coat that is somewhere <u>in between</u> the various tones of her face (not darker, not lighter) to smooth out any unevenness.

Flattering Palette: Using some 250-300 fabrics of various textures (cotton, silk, wool, velvet, etc.), we experiment with simultaneous contrast to determine specifically which hues (colors), values (dark-light), and intensities (dull-bright) create the appearance of a healthy, glowing complexion and bright and shining hair. If a color is merely "ho-hum" or if it takes more than five seconds to decide, we skip it. From each of the person's most complimentary colors we again cut a small piece, right then and there. I do not use any pre-cut group of color samples, as it would be irrelevant. Nor do I insist that my client fit neatly into one of four simple categories. Most of us "fall between the cracks."

Final Analysis: After accumulating 40-50 <u>best</u> color samples, I ask my client to arrange them in a logical sequence. Now, looking at her own color circle, we can EDIT, COMPARE and SEE how her own coloring is enhanced by this most flattering array! We also discuss design lines and wardrobe coordination.

SHOPPING MADE EASY!

I suggest that (at home) she mount the samples in the container that I provide (another excellent color exercise). Also, that she add a small card with a complete list of her measurements and a tape measure. Armed with such useful tools, regardless of poor lighting, absent mirrors and erratically sized garments, she can accomplish her shopping easily and quickly - <u>confident</u> that each piece she selects will look good on her as well as with each of the other pieces!

COMMON OPTICAL ILLUSIONS

With a **less-than-even complexion**: Small prints, checks or dots seem to keep right on going and spread over the face, emphasizing a splotchy appearance.

Dark colored circles beneath the eyes: Use concealer. Beware of repeating the same color in your eye shadow <u>above</u> the eyes; it creates the illusion of a racoon.

"Mousey" gray-blonde-brown hair: Browns of a <u>different</u> hue will make the hair appear to be the wrong color. Wear browns in the same color family as your own hair. The darkest tone will make your hair appear bright and shining, and the lightest tone will make your hair seem dark and rich. However, the medium tone may just be monotonous.

Sallow (yellow-grey) complexion: Most yellowish colors of any kind will echo and emphasize a sallow complexion. Sometimes a very vibrant aqua, blue or violet will intensify this sallow look, as well.

Any color, in the vicinity of its complement (its opposite on the color wheel) appears to become intensified.

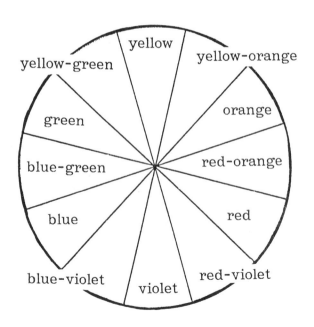

Keeping this in mind, when wearing even good near-violets, make certain you're wearing fresh blusher and lip color of a cool, pink-mauve tone or you may resemble a banana. **Rough, blotchy or sallow complexion**: Avoid smooth, glossy, pink-pink fabric. Comparison to the face is really not flattering. Almost anyone is going to look greenish-yellow when wearing greenish-yellow as this color is reflected on the face. By comparison, hot pink or the brightest fuschia next to a sallow skin may have the same effect because of strong contrast.

(However, the same type of illusion can be used to your advantage. Some aquas enhance a sun tan, some greens emphasize rosy cheeks and some violets make blonde hair appear more "golden.")

Face or hair will seem to disappear when surrounded by soft, greyed-pastels because those colors are so similar to the hue, intensity and value of the face and hair themselves. **Dull hair and complexions** seem downright dingy by comparison when placed next to intensely brilliant hues such as scarlet and citrus colors. **Pale face**: Black or very dark shades can cause a "ghost-like" appearance, by comparison. **"Peacock" apparel**: Some colors are so bright that people notice your jacket long before they notice that you're in it! Avoid this. The **color of your hair** is just as important as that of your complexion. Only select those values with sufficient contrast to highlight hair.

COLOR HARMONIES

The following two color harmonies are the most beautiful:

Strong contrast: A person with strong dramatic contrast in her own coloring, for instance, someone with black hair and very rosy cheeks or someone with rich warm brown skin, will often look dynamic in hues that are very intense. Conversely, a person with delicate coloring will usually be overpowered by such brilliance.

Closely related colors in evenly measured steps: This may take more skill to arrange, but the effort will create an effect of beauty as nothing else can! With the cheeks as the lightest tone of rose, for instance, and lips as the medium tone, try a blouse of deep rose! To heighten the effect, add a rose-burgundy skirt or pants. Now you have arranged a color "sequence" with your own face as an integral part of that sequence. Try it and see yourself glow!

HOW TO DESIGN YOUR WARDROBE

The purpose of clothing is to have it accomplish several things. It
- covers our nakedness
- keeps us warm
- protects our tender skin
- conveys status
- makes us look good

The last point may seem too basic even to mention. After all, few people select clothing to make themselves look bad!

And yet, that is sometimes exactly what we do. Here are some general rules for dressing for success.

Business wardrobe: When you are the newcomer, dress the way your boss, or your boss's boss, dresses. Find out if there's a company dress code, written or unwritten. Ultra conservative companies like I.B.M., for instance, are rather like the navy. They don't ask you if you look good in blue. You learn to wear a navy suit, white shirt, red tie and black shoes. You can like it or not. That's the way it is. I'm exaggerating a bit; but nevertheless, their dress code is unquestionably narrow.

As you feel more secure in your job, you can incorporate more individuality in your wardrobe.

Of course, by the time you are Chairman of the Board, you can wear anything you please.

The Professional Look: If uniforms are worn in your chosen profession, that will be your attire. Good grooming, naturally, is of the utmost importance. Start each day with clean, polished shoes in good repair, even hemlines, a spotless outfit with all buttons, seams and other details in good shape.

Office Clothing: Your professional look will usually include modest necklines and hem lines, covered arms, and either plain colors or quiet prints, rather than gaudy ones. Wear conservative jewelry, which should be real, if possible; otherwise, wear good costume jewelry.

279

Choose the finest natural-looking <u>fabric</u> that you can afford and can keep in good repair; wool, cotton, linen, rayon or silk either by themselves or combined with a synthetic for ease in cleaning. Invest in <u>shoes</u> of good quality leather as stylish as your budget, appropriateness to the job and comfort will allow. Quality leather shoes will enhance your overall appearance and are the best value because they look better and last longer than several pairs made of other materials. Comfort is important; plain shoes worn with a smile are infinitely more preferable than fancy footwear worn with an eternally pained frown.

Layers of coordinated garments will provide the most variety with the least amount of pieces for a total good look.

Fit: To appear as tall and as slim as possible, avoid clothing that is too tight. For unhindered movement, garments should fit correctly at the neck and shoulders, allowing ease at bicep, bust line, hip and thigh.

Style: Choose a style appropriate to your personality and your activities.

Proportion: Keep clothing detail and accessories in proportion to your body size.

Additional Hints: To appear tall and slim:
1. Wear the same color from shoulder to hem.
2. Wear either no belt at all, or wear a narrow belt of the same color as the garment.
3. Choose a softly gored, flared or pleated skirt, rather than a very narrow or very full one.
4. Have your jacket just long enough to

end at your largest circumference.
5. Match leg and footwear, such as long pants and shoes, skirts with long boots or matching shoes and hosiery.
6. Keep the high-contrast and attention-getting details of your garments near the face and shoulders.

In summary, the secret to looking your best on the outside is to be aware of the terrific and beautiful person you are on the inside. Then create your image accordingly.

Accentuate the positive and make the most of what you have!

48

HOW TO BUDGET
FOR YOUR FINANCIAL SECURITY

etting older isn't bad, when you consider the only alternative.

Being older won't be good, either . . . unless you plan ahead.

This plan must answer the questions:
- What do you have? (Income?)
- What do you need? (Expenses?)
- What do you want? (Goals?)
- How can you get it? (Steps to goals?)

INCOME

Only you know what you have. List on paper all your assets and income. (Live within that income.)

EXPENSES

Your needs should include:

- Living expenses
- Emergency savings which should amount to six months income, or enough to buy a new car.)
- Adequate insurance:
  Life: enough to cover death expenses, plus enough to tide the family over until the surviving spouse can provide sufficient income.
  Disability: if you are the wage earner.
  Health: total or enough to supplement Medicare.
  Homeowner's: Hint: Photograph belongings and save prints in safety deposit box.
  Auto: An absolute must.

GOALS

Here you can add any goal you like: a cottage by the sea, a sail to Tahiti, or income to provide you with the leisure time to write novels, paint landscapes, or create poetry.

STEPS TO ACHIEVE YOUR GOALS

- Invest in yourself: learn to earn. Pursue the education necessary to enable you to earn the best income that you can.
- **Live within that income!**
- **SAVE 10 percent or more of all that you earn!**
- Invest your savings; use savings accounts, money markets, growth stocks, and high-grade bonds, or other mediums. Consider mutual funds to spread the risk.

Yes, all of these entail risk. But, even if you do not invest, there is the risk that inflation and taxes may eat away your purchasing power.

Make your choice.

Recently, an average housewife's services were estimated at a value of $40,000 per year.

Without receiving cash wages, IF she were allowed to contribute (from her mate's wages) in her own name to Social Security, I.R.A., and/or a Keogh fund based on this she could build a retirement fund for herself.

As it is, we must work within the framework of the laws that exist, earn and save as much as possible. We must keep abreast of the latest legal changes and do the best we can to make our earnings work for us to earn more.

- -

ATTENTION!

If you do not already follow each of these "steps to achieve your goals," write them on a small piece of paper and carry that paper in a locket around your neck until you do!

49

TAKE CHARGE OF YOUR LIFE

fter all the talk, the ideas and the reflections, it boils down to this: Take charge of your life!

When you feel in control of your life, you are most satisfied with it.

Taking charge leads to feelings of strength and self-confidence.

Strength and self-confidence give you courage to risk new things.

Risking new things enables you to grow.

Growing empowers you to reach your greatest potential.

You can't give what you don't have.

It is only when you possess strength, self-confidence and satisfaction with your life, that you are able to give these things to others. When you improve your own life, you become more capable of enriching the lives of those around you.

Say to yourself, "I must start somewhere. The place is here. The time is now."

The first thing to do is to set down:

MY PERSONAL BILL OF RIGHTS

1. I am a person. As a person, I am due the same courtesy, consideration, attention, and respect as any other person.
2. I am entitled to my own feelings. They require no apology. I am entitled to conduct myself as best I can, being true to those feelings.
3. I owe it to myself to be the best person I can be. By developing myself, I am more capable of caring and sharing in a positive manner.
4. I owe it to my family and to myself, to see to it that they treat me, my time and my energy with the same respect, courtesy, attention, and consideration that they would accord anyone else. This means my goals are just as important as their goals.
5. I make the choice to be happy. Since I do have a choice, when I am asked to do things I do not wish to do, I must learn to say, simply, "No," rather than performing a service with grudging resentment. On the other hand, if there are chores which I must do, I will try my best to do them willingly and cheerfully.
6. It is my duty to make the most of my talents. To do less would be disrespectful to myself and be ungrateful to God.
7. I choose my own goals. I am not only free to do so; I must. Without goals, I have no direction and I merely drift without

purpose.

8. I must learn to take care of myself physically, intellectually, spiritually, psychologically, and financially. I cannot expect someone else to always do it for me.

9. I am responsible for my own actions. I cannot forever act as a child, awaiting permission to get on with my life. If I want something, I will have to work for it and make it happen!

10. I have the courage to try whatever I want to try. If I do not even try, I will never succeed. On the other hand, when I decide I really want something, I can intelligently prepare myself to pursue that goal with courage and perseverance.

I **CAN** DO IT!

. . . **AND I WILL!!**

Dear Reader:

Today you have finished reading "WOMEN AND SELF-CONFIDENCE . . ."

Now you know "how to take charge of your life."

It's up to you.

Begin now, striving to reach your greatest potential.

Build upon each new success, big or little, and let each accomplishment spur you on to the next.

As you grow and develop, I encourage you to be generous and share that success with others.

If you find that reading "WOMEN AND SELF-CONFIDENCE . . ." has helped you to take charge of your life and come closer to reaching your greatest potential, **let me know.**

I care about you. I am interested. And, I would like to help you share your successes with other women so that they, too, can be inspired to improve their lives.

When you write to me, let me know if you wish your personal success story to be included in my next book, "WOMEN AND SUCCESS," and whether or not you wish your name to be used.

This is what it's all about. By sharing the experience of your accomplishments, you can inspire others to strive to make **their** lives better, too.

So, show 'em how it's done!

And . . . **let me hear from you.**

Carol V. Havey

"WOMEN AND SELF-CONFIDENCE:
How to Take Charge of Your Life"

ORDER BLANK

Name _____

Mailing Address _____

City _____State ____ Zip _____

Please use this form to order additional copies of
"WOMEN AND SELF-CONFIDENCE . . ."

The price of each copy is $9.95 plus $1.09 for
shipping and handling (total $11.04/copy).
Note: Illinois residents need to include an additional $.70 for State sales tax (total $11.74/copy).

Number of copies ordered _____

Total amount enclosed: $_____

Make your check payable to: Positive Press
P.O. Box 3133
Joliet, IL 60436

GIFT PACKAGE AVAILABLE:

If you wish to send a gift copy to a friend,
please furnish her name and mailing address on
the back of the form. Her copy will be sent
with a special gift enclosure designed by the
author. Please indicate how you wish the enclosure to be inscribed.

Additional Reading Suggestions

SUCCESS

Positive Thinking

Carnegie, Dale
How to Stop Worrying & Start Living
Simon & Schuster, 1948
ISBN 06671556568

Carnegie, Dale
How to Win Friends & Influence People
Pocket (Simon & Schuster), 1981
ISBN 067146311X

Peale, Norman Vincent
Dynamic Imaging
Fleming H. Revell Co., 1982
ISBN 0800712781

Peale, Norman Vincent
Enthusiasm Makes the Difference
Prentice-Hall, Inc., 1967
Lib. of Cong. 67-26078

Creative Thinking

Koberg, Don and
Bagnall, Jim
The All New Universal Traveler:
a Soft Systems Guide to Creativity
and the Process of Reaching Goals
Wm. Kaufman, 1981 (paperback)
ISBN 0865760179

Von Oech, Roger
Whack on the Side of the Head
Warner Books, 1983 (paperback)
ISBN 0446382752

Goal Setting

Dyer, Wayne
Pulling Your Own Strings
Thos. Y. Crowell Co., 1978
ISBN 030810336X

Newman, Mildred and
Berkowitz, Bernard
How to Take Charge of Your Life
Harcourt, Brace, Jovanovich, 1977
ISBN 0151421927

Patent, Arnold M.
You Can Have It All
Money Mastery Pub., 1984
ISBN 0961366303

Sher, Barbara
Wishcraft
Viking Press, 1979
ISBN 0670776084

Time Management

Lakein, Alan
**How to Get Control of Your Time
and Your Life**
Wyden, 1973
Lib. of Cong. 73-75568

Clothing, Dress and Color for Success

August, Bonnie
**The Complete Bonnie August
Dress Thin System**
Rawson, Wade Pub., Inc., 1981
ISBN 0892561378

Bergen, Polly
I'd Love to, But What'll I Wear?
Wyden, 1977
ISBN 067122803X

Cho, Emily and
 Fisher, Neila
**It's You: Looking Terrific
Whatever Your Type**
Random. 1986
ISBN 039455129X

Head, Edith
How to Dress for Success
Random House, 1967
Lib. of Cong. 66-12021

Maron, Michael
Michael Maron's Instant Makeover Magic
Rawson Assoc., 1983
ISBN 089256234X

Marshall Editions, Ltd.
Color
Knapp Pub., 1980
ISBN 089350378

McJimsey, Harriet T.
Art and Fashion in Clothing Selection
Iowa State University Press, 1973
ISBN 0813801508

Wallach, Janet
Working Wardrobe
Acropolis Books, Ltd., 1981
ISBN 0874910722

WOMEN

Culture and Social Stratification of Women

Baruch, Grace,
  Barnett, Rosalind and
  Rivers, Caryl
Life Prints
McGraw-Hill, 1983
ISBN 0070529817

Catalyst, Inc.
What To Do With The Rest Of Your Life
Touchstone Books, 1981 (paperback)
ISBN 067125071X

Naisbitt, John
Megatrends
Warner, 1982 (paperback)
ISBN 0446909912

Sheehy, Gail
Pathfinders
Morrow, 1981
ISBN 0688006485

Women Workers

BPW: The National Federation of
     Business & Professional
     Women's Clubs
National Business Woman
Bimonthly magazine

Cunn, Rita & Kenneth
**How to Raise Independent &
Professionally Successful Daughters**
Prentice-Hall, Inc., 1977
ISBN 0134307100

Giele, Janet Zollinger
Women And The Future
Free Press, 1978
ISBN 0029117003

Lembeck, Ruth
Job Ideas for Today's Woman
Prentice-Hall, Inc., 1974
ISBN 0135100577

Magazines

Ms.
Savvy
Success
Working Woman

Women and Personal Finance

Ahern, Dee Dee and
  Bliss, Betsy
Economics of Being a Woman
MacMillon Pub. Co., Inc. 1976
ISBN 002500610X

Chesler, Phyllis and
  Goodman, E. J.
Women, Money & Power
Wm. Morrow & Co., Inc., 1976
ISBN 0688029907

Perkins, Gail and
  Rhoades, Judith
**The Women's Financial Survival
  Handbook**
Plume, 1983 (paperback)
ISBN 0452254108

Porter, Sylvia
**Sylvia Porter's New Money Book
  for the 80's**
Avon Books, 1980 (paperback)
ISBN 038051060X

Porter, Sylvia
Teach Your Wife To Be A Widow
Avon Books, 1979
Lib. Cong. 73-87354

Schlayer, Mary Eliz.
How To Be A Financially Secure Woman
Book Press, 1978
ISBN 0892560479

Women and Personal Management

Bolles, Rich
What Color Is Your Parachute?
Ten Speed Press, 1987 (paperback)
ISBN 0898151767

Corwen, Leonard
**Your Job - Where To Find It,
How To Get It**
Arco Pub., Inc., 1981
ISBN 0668051310

King, David and
Levine, Karen
**Best Way In The World For A Woman
To Make Money**
Warner Books, 1979
ISBN 044697515X

Women and Personal Success in Business

AARP News Bulletin
(American Association of Retired People)
Wash., D.C.

Azibo, Moni and
Unumb, Therese
Mature Woman's Back-To-Work Book
Contemporary Books, Inc., 1980
ISBN 0809270900 (paperback)

Catalyst Staff
Marketing Yourself
Bantam, 1981 (paperback)
ISBN 0553237519

Kleiman, Carol
Women's Networks
Lippincott & Crowell, Pub., 1980
ISBN 069001869X

Shook, Robert L.
Winning Images
MacMillon Pub. Co., Inc., 1977
ISBN 0026105463

Welsh, Mary Scott
Networking
Harcourt, Brace, Jovanovich, 1980
ISBN 015165199X

Home Based Business

Brabec, Barbara
Creative Cash
Aames-Allen, 1986 (paperback)
ISBN 0936930055

Crafts Report Publ. Co.
The Crafts Report
(Newsmonthly of Marketing, Management
and Money for Crafts Professionals)
700 Orange St.
Wilmington, DE 19801

Scott, Michael
The Crafts Business Encyclopedia
Harcourt, Brace, Jovanovich, 1977
ISBN 0151227527

Local Library
Valuable resource for all information
USE IT!

"WOMEN AND SELF-CONFIDENCE:
How to Take Charge of Your Life"

ORDER BLANK

Name _____

Mailing Address _____

City _____ State _____ Zip _____

Please use this form to order additional copies of "WOMEN AND SELF-CONFIDENCE . . ."

The price of each copy is $9.95 plus $1.09 for shipping and handling (total $11.04/copy).
Note: Illinois residents need to include an additional $.70 for State sales tax (total $11.74/copy).

Number of copies ordered _____

Total amount enclosed: $_____

Make your check payable to: Positive Press
P.O. Box 3133
Joliet, IL 60436

GIFT PACKAGE AVAILABLE:

If you wish to send a gift copy to a friend, please furnish her name and mailing address on the back of the form. Her copy will be sent with a special gift enclosure designed by the author. Please indicate how you wish the enclosure to be inscribed.

158

About the Author

Photograph by Chris Havey

DISCARD

Carol Havey has discovered that merely feeling good is not enough; you need to feel good about yourself.

This Chicago nurse, wife, homemaker and mother of seven, draws upon her additional expertise as personal color counselor, fashion designer, portrait artist, entrepreneur, lecturer and writer to show how to increase your self-confidence, make the most of your assets and become the very best YOU that you can be!